WARRIOR 171

SOVIET PARTISAN 1941–44

NIK CORNISH   ILLUSTRATED BY ANDREI KARACHTCHOUK

Series editor Marcus Cowper

First published in Great Britain in 2014 by Osprey Publishing,
PO Box 883, Oxford, OX1 9PL, UK
PO Box 3985, New York, NY 10185-3985, USA
E-mail: info@ospreypublishing.com

© 2014 Osprey Publishing Ltd

OSPREY PUBLISHING IS PART OF THE OSPREY GROUP.

A CIP catalogue record for this book is available from the British Library.

ISBN: 978 1 4728 0143 2
E-book ISBN: 978 1 4728 0145 6
PDF ISBN: 978 1 4728 0144 9

Editorial by Ilios Publishing Ltd, Oxford, UK (www.iliospublishing.com)
Index by Zoe Ross
Typeset in Myriad Pro and Sabon
Artwork by Andrei Karachtchouk
Originated by PDQ Media, UK
Printed in China through Worldprint Ltd.

14 15 16 17 18 10 9 8 7 6 5 4 3 2 1

Osprey Publishing is supporting the Woodland Trust, the UK's leading
woodland conservation charity, by funding the dedication of trees.

www.ospreypublishing.com

DEDICATION

This book is dedicated to the men and women of the Soviet partisan
movement, whatever their origin or belief and to my family; Mum Dorothy,
Angie, Charlotte, Alex and James.

ACKNOWLEDGEMENTS

To everyone who helped with this book, particularly Dmitry Belanovsky
and Norbert Hofer – thank you.

ARTIST'S NOTE

Readers may care to note that the original paintings from which the colour
plates in this book were prepared are available for private sale. The Publishers
retain all reproduction copyright whatsoever. All enquiries should be
addressed to:

a.karaschuk@gmail.com

The Publishers regret that they can enter into no correspondence upon
this matter.

CONTENTS

INTRODUCTION 4

CHRONOLOGY 7

RECRUITMENT 9

TRAINING 13

ORGANIZATION 17

APPEARANCE 19

EQUIPMENT 24

CONDITIONS OF SERVICE 30

ON CAMPAIGN 37

BELIEF AND BELONGING 41

EXPERIENCE OF BATTLE 46

AFTER THE BATTLE 60

MUSEUMS AND COLLECTIONS 61

BIBLIOGRAPHY 62

GLOSSARY 63

INDEX 64

SOVIET PARTISAN 1941–44

INTRODUCTION

The Soviet partisan movement during World War II has rarely been the subject of popular study in the West. In part this is as a result of four factors: an ignorance of its true scale, a lack of accessible information, a lack of the horrific glamour of a Kursk or a Stalingrad and, finally, many Westerners' perception of what partisan warfare was all about – these were not chic French ladies saucily defacing Hitler's portrait. The partisan war in the west was a very different one to that in the east and the portrayal of both in the media leaves much to be desired.

Where it has been referred to in general histories of the war on the Eastern Front information has often been plucked from memoirs or official Soviet accounts. These frequently credit the partisans with tying down hundreds of thousands of Axis troops and destroying hundreds of tanks to the extent that the reader is left wondering how the Germans got to the Volga at all with all this going on in their rear. Consequently the degree of artistic and historical licence taken has had the unfortunate effect of trivializing perceptions of what was a hellish day-to-day struggle for many thousands of combatants. Hitler commented in 1941 that the war in the east would not be fought in a 'knightly fashion'. This was racial war that included not only the Jews and the Poles but the Slav population of the USSR as well – in the name of *Lebensraum* genocide was the order of the day.

This book does not cover the partisan war or the occupation policies of the Third Reich: it looks at the partisans' way of life and how it was lived. Much of the information is drawn from interviews carried out by the author a decade ago. Two of the interviewees, Dr Albert Tsessarsky and Boris Chorny fought in the 'Winners' partisan unit under Colonel D. N. Medvedev.

Both were happy to recall their experiences without stressing the more horrific aspects of partisan warfare. Indeed Tsessarsky had written a memoir that, on publication during the Communist era, had led to him being censured for 'making Tsar Nicholas II appear to be human'. He also wrote of his own experiences in *The Diaries of a Partisan Doctor* in which he described Kuznetsov, a Soviet hero of the partisan war, as he really was. Consequently Tsessarsky was summoned to the Lubyanka building (the secret police HQ since the days of the Cheka) in Moscow where the KGB told him that he must write 'not as it was, but as it should be'. This sentence is telling as it describes much of what was written about the Soviet partisan war following 1945 and the mythologizing of the war behind Axis lines in the area known as 'the Temporarily Occupied Territories' or the 'Little Land'.

Background

Between 1939 and 1941 the USSR had reoccupied parts of western Ukraine and western Belarus as well as the Baltic states, part of Finland and Bessarabia. A policy of Russification and Sovietization had rapidly been carried out in these areas, which led to an upsurge in anti-Russian feeling that in turn fostered an embryonic pro-German, pro-nationalist resistance movement. It was against these groups as well as the Axis security formations that Soviet partisan groups would be fighting in the years following the invasion of the USSR in 1941. Consequently when the Red Army rolled the invaders back to the suburbs of Warsaw and into East Prussia during 1944 the myth of one people standing firm in adversity had to be cemented into fact.

The fact that Ukrainian and other citizens of the expanded USSR had fought what amounted to a civil war first against the Soviet partisans and then the Red Army was scrupulously overlooked. Rapidly the legend that all civilians in the 'Little Land' were partisans became an accepted truth. Neither Chorny nor Tsessarsky skirted away from the issue of fighting collaborators or nationalists; both commented that they lost more comrades fighting the nationalists than they did the Axis. Nor did they regard their actions with anything other than justifiable pride and were pleased to be able to contribute the stories of their participation in their country's involvement in the struggle for victory.

Following the Russian Civil War Soviet popular culture had emphasized the role of the ordinary civilian who fought for the Communist cause, either as a member of the Red Army or an irregular. Indeed, the latter were glorified in books, poems and films such as *Chapaev* released to much acclaim and playing to packed cinemas across the USSR in 1934. Russia's history was peppered with tales of peasant uprisings, while the irregular warfare conducted against Napoleon's *Grande Armée* as it retreated from Moscow was the stuff of legend. Therefore the concept of partisan warfare had a clearly understood and acceptable place in Stalin's empire. However, the very characteristics that made for a good partisan, and particularly a good partisan

Nestor Makhno, facing the camera, the legendary anarchist partisan leader of the Russian Civil War and members of his staff. A master of swift attacks in unexpected places followed by a rapid disengagement to attack elsewhere and blessed with a charismatic personality, Makhno was the embodiment of the word *Partisanshchina*. (Courtesy of the Central Museum of the Armed Forces Moscow via www.stavka.org.uk)

leader, were not traits that made for a good Soviet citizen. Abilities such as thinking independently, acting swiftly without automatic reference to higher authority, inspiring others, resourcefulness and the possession of an indefinable charismatic 'something' were not desirable in the post-purge Soviet Union where keeping one's head down and avoiding criticism was what counted. The Russian word *Partisanshchina* sums up the qualities of a good partisan but suggests a certain deviation from the norms of society that is not altogether appropriate or desirable.

Indeed, in the realm of military theory the very concept of partisan warfare was one that it was no longer fashionable or safe to discuss. Throughout the 1920s and into the 1930s partisan operations had been an accepted part of Soviet strategy, with the assumption that the next war would, initially, be fought on Soviet territory. Units would be expected to attack enemy supply lines, lines of communications and disrupt their rear areas as much as possible. To carry out these operations secret bases were to be established deep in the forests and marshlands of the border regions. Stalin, increasingly suspicious of the military establishment from the early 1930s, decided that the offensive was now preferable to the defensive and that the next war would be fought exclusively on enemy soil, which effectively rendered preparations for partisan warfare pointless. The result was that plans for bases and the like were shelved indefinitely; conventional warfare was the order of the day.

When the storm broke and Operation *Barbarossa* rendered pre-war Soviet planning obsolete, and as the Red Army reeled under a series of hammer blows, the leadership cast around for any potentially effective means of stemming the invaders' march to the east.

On 3 July 1941 Stalin broadcast to a stunned nation. Frankly admitting that territory had been lost, he called for a scorched earth policy in the face of the enemy, while behind their lines he called for the following:

During the summer of 1941 hundreds of thousands of Red Army troops were captured and sent to the rear in weakly guarded columns from which escape was simple. It was men such as these that became known as the *Okruzhentsy*. Concealment was easier in Belarus due to the thick woods and marshes but, in Ukraine, the rolling, often featureless steppe was difficult to hide in. (Nik Cornish@ www.stavka.org.uk)

In areas occupied by the enemy guerrilla units, mounted and on foot must be formed, diversionist groups must be organized to combat enemy troops to foment guerrilla warfare everywhere, to blow up bridges and roads, damage telephone and telegraph lines, set fire to forests, stores, transports. In the occupied regions conditions must be made unbearable for the enemy and all his accomplices. They must be hounded and annihilated at every step and all their measures frustrated... All forces of the people for the demolition of the enemy.

The aggressors were obviously the Germans and their Romanian, Hungarian, Italian and Slovakian allies. The victims, in Stalin's words, included 'Russians, Ukrainians, Belorussians, Lithuanians, Latvians, Moldavians, Georgians, Estonians ... and the other free people of the Soviet Union'. The people had been called to war, Stalin himself had sanctioned a partisan campaign, it now remained for them to be organized in the Unoccupied Territories or, as they became known, the 'Great Land'.

CHRONOLOGY

22 June 1941	Operation *Barbarossa*, the German invasion of the Soviet Union, begins.
Summer–autumn 1941	German security reports indicate significant partisan activity mainly undertaken by isolated groups of Red Army men.
27 June 1941	The Ukrainian Communist Party issues orders for partisan warfare.
June 1941	Tsessarsky and Chorny volunteer for military service.
3 July 1941	Stalin calls for guerrilla war.
5 July 1941	The NKVD (People's Commissariat for Internal Affairs) begins to recruit for the Independent/Separate Special Purpose Motorized Rifle Brigade (the acronym for which was OMSBON).
28 July 1941	The Central Committee of the Communist Party issues detailed instructions to regional Party leaders ordering them to organize resistance themselves.
Summer 1941	S. A. Kovpak begins to organize a partisan unit in Putivl, north-west Ukraine.
July–November 1941	Regional partisan staffs formed in Karelia, Crimea, Ukraine, Leningrad and Moscow. There is no umbrella organization to co-ordinate these efforts.
Late summer 1941	Large numbers of non-Russian (particularly Ukrainian and Caucasian) POWs released by the Axis provided they 'work usefully for the Reich'. Of those that return to their homes many slip off to join the partisans. However, large numbers adopt a 'wait and see' attitude.
Late September 1941	Widespread destruction in central Kiev (occupied by Germans 19 September) by NKVD operatives.
October–December 1941	Chorny and Tsessarsky deploy with OMSBON to defend Moscow.
1941–44	Fighting between Ukrainian, Baltic, Polish nationalist groups and pro-Soviet partisans. These nationalist

	groups were not necessarily pro-Nazi/fascist but regard Axis forces as the lesser evil of two totalitarian systems.
Winter 1941–42	The partisan movement reaches its lowest ebb due to lack of supplies, shelter, a central organisation to oversee the groups' welfare and an impossible climate in which to survive.
Early 1942	Chorny and Tsessarsky begin partisan-specific training with other members of OMSBON.
Autumn–winter 1941–42	The realities of Hitler's occupation policies begin to become apparent.
30 May 1942	The establishment in Moscow of the Central HQ for the Partisan Movement (CHQPM) to co-ordinate and control the entire Soviet partisan structure other than NKVD units.
Spring 1942	Himmler insists that the word bandit replace that of partisan in all official communications. This is a deliberate attempt to remove the military overtones associated with partisans and thereby outlaw them.
August–September 1942	Highpoint of Axis advance into the Soviet Union. The Stalingrad campaign begins. Partisan units in Belarus and Ukraine ordered to intercept trains heading for Stalingrad.
Spring 1943	One of the effects of victory at Stalingrad is an upsurge in partisan recruitment and support.
July–October 1943	Operation *Rail War* and Operation *Concert* carried out to disrupt the German withdrawal following their defeat at the battle of Kursk. Both partisan operations were on a scale not attempted before.
Spring–autumn 1943	Kovpak's March in western Ukraine beginning what became known as the Carpathian Raid.
Autumn 1943	Official termination of the Carpathian Raid.
Autumn–winter 1943	A significant upsurge in partisan recruitment sows the seeds of mistrust between the veterans and the newcomers.
Winter 1943–44	The partisan movement in the Leningrad region contributes significantly to the Red Army's offensive to drive Heeresgruppe Nord back into the Baltic States.
13 January 1944	The CHQPM is disbanded and responsibility for the partisan movement devolves on the Party organization in each Soviet republic.
Spring 1944	Planning for Operation *Bagration*, the liberation of Belarus, begins. The partisans are to be fully involved gathering intelligence and undertaking specific sabotage missions. They will also be involved in combat supporting the Red Army in more significant numbers than ever before.
22 June 1944	Operation *Bagration* begins. Almost everyone in Belarus considers themselves to be partisans.
17 July	Partisans parade through Minsk. Amateur units begin to demobilize and are conscripted into the Red Army, the professionals are sent to other areas.

RECRUITMENT

Broadly speaking, membership of the partisan movement fell into two categories: professionals (members of the armed forces) and amateurs (civilians), and which came first is difficult, if not impossible, to discover. Doubtless there was a civilian who shot at German troops during the first week of the invasion prior to Stalin's call for guerrillas but, unfortunately, no name has been found. The Ukrainian Communist Party (then led by N. S. Khrushchev) announced a partisan war in late June 1941, but this is possibly a case of Khrushchev inflating his own importance following Stalin's death. Consequently, it would appear that the professional partisan was first in the field. As early as 25 June, Heeresgruppe Mitte, heading eastwards through Belarus, reported that 'stragglers and guerrillas' were attacking supply convoys, field hospitals and security troops. These partisans generally consisted of isolated groups of Red Army men trying to fight their way back to their own lines and do some damage on the way, and were known as the *Okruzhentsy*. As communications had virtually broken down there was little chance that such groups could contact their own forces and also, given the speed of the German advance, it was well nigh impossible to re-join them. Consequently their only option was to wait in the forests and marshes of Belarus and see what happened. Groups of stragglers frequently coalesced into larger formations under an NCO, officer or political commissar/officer (*Politruk*). When and where it was safe to do so others faded into the population. Certainly in western Belarus, western Ukraine and the Baltic States that was a very dangerous choice to make as so many of the population were anti-Russian and would happily turn in Red Army stragglers to the Germans.

Simultaneously, the Party and the NKVD were also recruiting men and women for their own partisan groups. Fifteen days after Stalin's call to arms the Central Committee of the Communist Party issued detailed instructions to its regional organizations regarding partisan formations. Partisan units were to be recruited from 'particularly reliable leading Party, Soviet and *Komsomol* members and also non-Party individuals devoted to the Soviet regime'. Their local knowledge was vital as they were ordered to 'destroy the

Recruitment was not only a matter for the individual concerned, it also impacted on the family. Those left behind were at risk from informers, registration of population checks or a simple slip of the tongue. As partisan power grew so did the sometimes coercive nature of their recruitment drives, which pressured the less willing into their ranks. (Courtesy of the Central Museum of the Armed Forces Moscow via www.stavka.org.uk)

hoarders and their collaborators'. These volunteer formations were divided into companies, platoons and sections along the lines of the Red Army. The luckier groups would benefit from the experience of veterans of World War I or the Russian Civil War rather than Party hacks or bureaucrats foisted on them from above.

One such group was formed in Putivl, north-east of Kiev in rural Ukraine, by the 55-year-old Sidor Artemyevitch Kovpak, a veteran of both World War I (during which he won four important awards for outstanding bravery) and the Russian Civil War, during which he had fought under Chapaev's command. Following demobilization Kovpak had devoted himself to local politics in the Sumy region where Putivl was located. Clearly a Party loyalist, with an impeccable record, by 1941 he had risen to become Chairman of the Party's district committee, a powerful and influential position.

Kovpak's force numbered some 50 men, mainly government employees and Party workers. The unit took to the nearby Spadshchansky Forest and the surrounding marshy wilderness before the Germans occupied Putivl on 10 September. Within days they were joined by a group of stragglers, men of an airborne unit that had escaped the encirclement of Kiev. During this time hundreds of other Red Army men were guided westwards by locals, singly or in groups, as they attempted to re-join their units. In early October another local partisan leader, S. V. Rudnev, merged his force with that of Kovpak. Rudnev was a former Red Army political commissar and he assumed this role in the newly combined force, which, by the end of 1941, numbered some 400–500 fighters. From this time onwards, however, membership of partisan formations such as this became progressively stricter as the risk of infiltration by individual collaborators or the assimilation of German-organized 'partisan' groups increased. Prospective members were placed on probation and their movements monitored until their bona fides could be checked. If a partisan unit possessed a radio a call would be made to Moscow and the aspirant would be, if possible, investigated. A negative reply generally led to summary execution.

Kovpak's force was not unique in accepting deserters from their opponents. During the summer of 1942 eight Ruthenians, conscripted into the Hungarian Army, joined the partisans and fought 'as good friends and brave soldiers'. Also one or two members of the Légion des Volontaires Français, a German-sponsored French unit engaged in security duties, deserted to Kovpak in 1942. In the aftermath of Stalingrad other deserters joined the partisans although they appear to have been mainly Slovaks and Hungarians.

In addition to the Communist Party itself, the NKVD recruited for two formations. To the west of Moscow the provincial staffs organized the dramatically entitled 'destruction battalions' that were tasked with rear-area security – a broad remit. Members of these units were drawn exclusively from the uniformed NKVD, which included the frontier guard, the police and some 30 operational divisions modelled on army rifle divisions. These battalions were to complete any outstanding destruction of strategic facilities such as bridges or railway depots following the withdrawal of the Red Army, before changing into civilian dress and waging war on the enemy and collaborators. However, it was the Moscow-based NKVD unit that was to come to greater prominence during the next three years – the Separate Special Purpose Motorized Rifle Brigade (OMSBON).

Attempts to dissuade civilians from joining the partisans were brutally unsubtle. Three alleged partisans are seen here on their way to be publicly executed because, as the notice around the woman's neck reads, 'We are partisans, we shot at German soldiers'. (Courtesy of the Central Museum of the Armed Forces Moscow via www.stavka.org.uk)

Recruitment for this formation was quite remarkable as it included, from the outset, a wide variety of nationalities – including some 2,000 political exiles from the USA, Germany, Spain, Poland, Vietnam and Romania. It was deemed essential that recruits be physically capable of enduring life in swamps and forests where surviving on short rations was the norm. Consequently many were sportsmen, such as players in the NKVD football teams Dynamo Minsk and Dynamo Moscow – the former having been sent en masse to the capital two days before Minsk fell. Hundreds of volunteers from the army's sports club CSKA came forward as did personnel from the NKVD's administration in Moscow. Numbers of NKVD frontier guard were also drafted in.

Boris Chorny was employed by the NKVD as a film projectionist at the Central Club of the NKVD in Moscow. Chorny attempted to volunteer on the day that war was declared but was informed that on account of his job his service was deferred. Then, unexpectedly, he was told that he was eligible for service in OMSBON. Following his training Chorny decided that he would like to join Medvedev's partisan unit 'Mitya' (which preceded the 'Winners') as it was well known for its activities behind enemy lines. At interview Medvedev asked Chorny what he could do to which he answered 'shoot and parachute jump'. These attributes were insufficient, but Medvedev's political commissar was a friend of Chorny and got him in as a guard. As Chorny recalled, 'It was so hard to get an opportunity to die for your Motherland'.

Another Muscovite was medical student Albert Tsessarsky. Along with friends in the *Komsomol*, Tsessarsky was eager to volunteer for the front. He was ordered to attend at the Central Committee of the *Komsomol* where he joined hundreds of other students from different academic institutions in Moscow. Selected members of the *Komsomol* were being considered for assignment to OMSBON. Tsessarsky remembered sitting in an anteroom listening to various conversations, in particular one pair discussing the

Обявление!
ЗА ПОЙМАННОГО "БАНДИТА "КАТЮ"
Германское Командование
ВОЗНАГРАДИТ: ПОЙМАВШЕГО :
3.000 МАРОК : 5 ПУДОВ СОЛИ, А ТАКЖЕ
ЗЕМЕЛЬНЫМ НАДЕЛОМ В 25 ГЕКТАР
Ortskommandantür Dobrusch
Комендант Добручского района:
Обермейтенант Брокман

When coercion failed cupidity was a widely used incentive for would be informers. The poster offered, '3,000 Marks, 5 *pouds* (82kg) of salt and a 25 hectare plot of land, as a reward for the capture of the bandit Katya'. The allocation of such an area of land would have pointed a finger directly at the informer with fatal consequences. (From the fonds of the RGAKFD, Kranogorsk via www.stavka.org.uk)

relative merits of the poetry of Blok and Kipling. The two students in question later served together in what became known as the 'company of philosophers', which was renowned for its devotion to the Communist Party and for its political maturity.

If Kovpak became leader of his unit for his proven political and military track record then Dmitry Nikolayevich Medvedev was chosen for his quite remarkable personality. Born near Bryansk in 1898 he had fought in the Civil War, becoming a Communist Party member and Cheka employee in 1920. By 1936 he had risen to the rank of Chief Inspector of the NKVD for the Kharkov region. However, he was expelled from the Party and the NKVD in 1937 as he disagreed with the NKVD's role in the Purges. At this point he took himself off to the Kursk railway station in Moscow and telegraphed Stalin announcing he was on hunger strike. Due to his previously exemplary record he avoided the firing squad and was posted to work at a labour camp near the Arctic Circle. Once again he upset his superiors for releasing unconvicted prisoners and was retired on the grounds of ill health.

When war broke out Medvedev went to the Lubyanka, the HQ of the secret services from the time of the Cheka to the KGB, and asked to be appointed head of a partisan unit, preferably in his home district of Bryansk west of Moscow. Having been kept waiting for a week he was sent to lead a destruction battalion codenamed 'Mitya' near Smolensk, which he did until January 1942. During those months he built up a reputation for ruthless efficiency, organizational ability and charismatic leadership – the very embodiment of *Partisanshchina*.

However, the majority of the population under Axis control viewed the partisans as a mixed blessing. There were vast areas that had suffered under Stalin's collectivization policies, particularly in Ukraine; to many therefore the German occupation was greeted as an opportunity that might lead to the re-distribution of land and the reinstatement of private property. Consequently many adopted a neutral stance, hoping privately for an improvement in their way of life. In some areas freedom of worship was reinstated and a degree of local political autonomy allowed. However, it was only when the realities of German racial and occupation policies, such as the deportation of workers to the Reich, food levies and genocide, became day to day occurrences that the attitudes of many of the people of the 'Little Land' began to change and voluntary recruitment figures for the partisans grew. In the wake of the Axis defeat at Stalingrad, new members began to come forward as the partisan units themselves spread news of Soviet victories, as they were the only organizations that could access information from Moscow. Following the failed German summer offensive at Kursk during July 1943 another wave of recruits presented themselves. By early 1944 the partisan information and propaganda machine was drawing in more recruits than it was capable of dealing with and resentment began to build between those recently enrolled and those who had served in the early days. Recruitment was therefore restricted to those deemed worthy or particularly useful. Indeed, as the Red Army moved westwards the civilian-based partisan groups were conscripted wholesale whereas the NKVD formations were placed deeper into occupied territory, often beyond the borders of the USSR. During Operation *Bagration*, which resulted in the speedy liberation of Belarus and western Ukraine, thousands who had remained sitting on the fence rapidly armed themselves and went 'Fritz hunting' for stragglers as German units dissolved in the chaotic conditions that ensued before the front line was re-established in front of Warsaw.

TRAINING

In theory all mentally and physically able males were, at the age of 19, eligible for conscription into the armed forces. There were several categories of exemption such as specialist workers or those deemed unworthy of bearing arms by dint of close family members being enemies of the state. Many conscripts would have received very basic semi-military training at school or as members of the Union of Societies of Assistance to Defence and Aviation and Chemical Defence and Chemical Industry (OSOAVIAKhIM), the state organization that aimed to give a 'patriotic upbringing [to] the population and [prepare] it for the defence of the Motherland'. It did this by providing paramilitary training, via sports clubs, to young people. By 1941 it boasted some 13 million members across the USSR. Although membership was supposedly voluntary it was effectively mandatory for members of the *Komsomol* or for anyone aspiring to higher education. Clubs existed to give training in parachuting, gliding, marksmanship, driving, radiotelegraphy and horsemanship all with a view to providing a pool of reserve, part-trained military specialists. OSOAVIAKhIM owned its rifle ranges and airfields and Boris Chorny was a member of such a parachuting club near Moscow.

However, such facilities were not always accessible to the rural population. Hunting was a popular and necessary activity in the countryside, which in turn led to the development of skills such as marksmanship, concealment, stealthy movement and, above all, patience. Clearly such attributes were essential to life in a partisan group. The opportunities to gain such abilities were limited for 'city boys', as Tsessarsky described himself and his

The winter of 1941–42 was hellish for the partisans and dissuaded many potential recruits. Despite the weather and the lack of organization to support them they continued to carry out acts of sabotage. This group is shown destroying telegraph lines alongside a railway line and carrying off the wires. Activities such as this provided evidence for the Soviet authorities to use as propaganda for the ongoing struggle against the enemy in the 'Temporarily Occupied Territories'. (Courtesy of the Central Museum of the Armed Forces Moscow via www.stavka.org.uk)

compatriots. Nevertheless, when war broke out there was a considerable pool of potential recruits with a rudimentary knowledge of military life and a wide variety of experiences to contribute to a partisan formation.

Of course most of the military personnel would have received training appropriate to their branch of service. However, small unit training in the pre-war Red Army had been poor – men and officers below the rank of battalion commander were tacitly discouraged from displaying initiative; they were to follow orders and not generate too many ideas. Only officers and NCOs received training in map reading and the use of a compass. The two-year conscription period did not include much in the way of training related to operations in deep forests or marshland in the hit and run manner of the partisan. Battles would be fought on open ground with space to manoeuvre. However, there was one group of regular soldiers who found the less-formal style of warfare an easy adjustment, the *razvedchiki*, the elite infantry scouts. Each infantry regiment grouped its most suitable men into scouting companies, which could be consolidated into a battalion at divisional level. The training of these men was very much in line with the requirements of partisan warfare. Their duties included infiltrating enemy positions to gather information on their dispositions, unit identification, scouting enemy defensive positions and the taking of prisoners for interrogation. The scouts were expected to show initiative and guile while carrying out their missions, operate without direct supervision in small groups, live off of the land, be expert exponents of field craft, ruthless and efficient killers with a variety of weapons and be sufficiently trustworthy not to desert when behind enemy lines.

Amongst the military-style NKVD units the frontier guards were the best equipped to deal with the partisan way of life and combat. Furthermore they were politically reliable and loyal. They operated along the borders of the USSR where the opportunities for the interdiction of counter-revolutionaries, smugglers, people traffickers and other such anti-Soviet elements abounded, particularly during the years 1939–41, when the Soviet Union absorbed millions of Poles, Balts, Finns and Romanians due to the westward movement of the USSR's borders. This western buffer zone gave the frontier guards a prime opportunity to hone their skills in what was slowly developing into an anti-partisan campaign, particularly in occupied Poland.

Initial training for Chorny and Tsessarsky with the OMSBON proved to be a less than interesting experience. Both were exempt from conscription and therefore had little more than their school and club experiences to prepare them for the realities of military life.

Chorny, having convinced the authorities that he was suitable for a military career, began his training in July 1941 at various locations in and

around Moscow. The summer of 1941 'was a very hot one' and he remembered that as a consequence of the heat they only trained for two hours a day. There were very strict rules about respecting senior officers and Chorny recalled his embarrassment at vigorously saluting a splendidly uniformed railway official by mistake. Their tented training camp was on the outskirts of Moscow and on one occasion Chorny was ordered to visit a nearby village to practice his intelligence-gathering skills by finding out how many men of military age lived there. Disguised as a woman he approached a local and asked, 'Were there any officers in town?' The response is unprintable and he had a great deal of difficulty convincing his irate attacker that he was not a spy. As rifles were in short supply weapons training did not begin until September 1941. Chorny and his colleagues were very pleased as this new work cut down the time spent on etiquette and square bashing.

Practicing with Molotov cocktails as they were irreverently known. The politically acceptable name was 'bottle with flammable mixture'. Although 'flammable mixture' was fairly readily available in urban areas it was rarer out in the countryside where mines were more accessible. (Courtesy of the Central Museum of the Armed Forces Moscow via www.stavka.org.uk)

Route marches in all kinds of weather were an indispensable part of OMSBON's training regime. Note the unarmed woman second from right. Female members of partisan units were expected to be as physically fit as the men. (Courtesy of the Central Museum of the Armed Forces Moscow via www.stavka.org.uk)

Tsessarsky described his early weeks in much the same way. However, for him and other medical students priority was given to engender the skills related to battlefield surgery, diet in the field, herbal medication and psychology – much emphasis was placed on the ability of the individual to cope with battlefield stress and the strangeness of partisan life. Of particular concern was the need to be able to pack up and move rapidly. Medical units were instructed to be ready to 'curl up and leave in three to five minutes'. Furthermore they practised using the minimum of equipment and learnt to improvise what they lacked. Medical personnel were expected to train combat troops in basic first aid but this was not carried out in the classroom, it was done under field conditions during training exercises: 'We returned tired, wet and dirty but did not go to the barracks.' Unexpected night exercises were often called; and, as the front was approaching Moscow, no one dared to take them for granted. One night Tsessarsky's platoon was summoned to arms and told that enemy paratroopers had been spotted in a nearby wood. 'We tried to move as quietly as possible, but we did not succeed. Under my feet twigs crunched. The forest that we [passed] along and across on daily tactical exercises at night seemed unfamiliar and hostile. We saw nothing [only] heard, as heavy as asthmatics, our neighbours' breathing.' After a nerve-wracking night the operation, as 'it turned out, was a test of our readiness. These alarms were repeated almost every night. Soldiers have to learn.'

However, when the OMSBON troops returned from their deployment in defence of Moscow their partisan-specific training began in earnest. Tsessarsky remembered 'whole days were spent hiking through the woods. We learnt how to use a compass, we staged ambush training.' Map reading was also included. All under the direction of experienced officers 'who have returned from their first tasks'. These officers 'shared [tested] methods of training with [anti-]personnel mines, explosive charges under the rails and camouflage. Classes were held at night [on] the highways and Moscow railways. Much attention was paid to ski and parachute training.'

For those already behind enemy lines training was less theoretical and more fraught with danger. Training for the amateurs that joined Kovpak during the summer of 1941 was a limited experience and fairly typical of that undertaken by similar units in threatened areas. There was no square bashing, little or no practical weapons training, quite a few political lectures and some specific courses in demolition, although these were often curtailed due to lack of equipment. In part this was due to a belief that if their territory was occupied it would only be for a short time. Despite Stalin's call for a partisan war it was politically unwise to consider a long war let alone defeat; indeed, regular officers were being executed on a daily basis for retreating without orders. Defeatism was a capital offence and there were sufficient NKVD operatives to ensure that defeatists were

An anonymous partisan unit trains with a 50mm mortar M40 and the M1910 Maxim machine gun. In the distance the riflemen appear to be advancing in staggered line over very open terrain. (Courtesy of the Central Museum of the Armed Forces Moscow via www.stavka.org.uk)

dealt with swiftly. Nevertheless, the propaganda notwithstanding, the Red Army did fall back beyond Ukraine and suddenly Kovpak and his men were de facto partisans. It was only when they attempted to lift some mines that they found out that the model scattered in profusion in the surrounding area was not the one about which they had been lectured. The situation was similar with other weapons. Some men were former soldiers and thus familiar with rifles, possibly the Maxim machine gun and an older type of hand grenade. But now that the war was in deadly earnest their training would have to be on the job. They were very lucky to merge with a group of paratroopers who were able to bring up-to-date weapons experience, which they were willing to share with the amateurs. But to avoid making too much noise, practice had to be in the nature of dry-firing: combat would be the best training these men would undergo and this would leave little margin for error.

Weapons training with a senior lieutenant. The summer of 1941 was hot and activities were curtailed to avoid heat exhaustion. Lucky were the recruits that actually had weapons to train with as many units just used sticks for marching drill. (Courtesy of the Central Museum of the Armed Forces Moscow via www.stavka.org.uk)

ORGANIZATION

OMSBON was organized as a military unit from the outset. It consisted of the 1st and 2nd Motorised Rifle Regiments, each of which, roughly 1,000 men, was divided into three battalions of four companies of four platoons split into four sections. When the brigade was distributed behind enemy lines it did so in sections that contained specialists of all types, from sappers to scouts and signallers, drawn from the appropriate companies of the battalion or regiment. Between 1941 and 1945 some 20,000 personnel passed through

An NKVD Frontier Guard shows one method of firing from behind cover. Specialists such as this mounted scout were often employed to demonstrate their skills. Many partisan units mounted their scout platoons. The scouts were regarded as an elite due to their mastery of the refinements of partisan warfare. (Nik Cornish@ www.stavka.org.uk)

its ranks. As well as infantry formations, its structure from 1943 included specialist anti-tank, demolition, mortar, logistics and communications companies as well as a paratrooper unit. These were deployed on specific missions where and when the need arose or as replacements for units, such as the 'Winners', that were already in the field.

However, the amateur partisan units generally grew from small cadres into what, by 1942, resembled military formations. The basic component was the section, several of which formed a platoon; four platoons constituted a company and four companies equalled a battalion. During 1942–43 most battalions were part of a brigade system organized by the CHQPM. Specialists, such as machine-gunners and sappers, originally organized at a platoon level, often developed into self-contained units. Radio operators were part of the HQ staff and their highly prized equipment was rarely loaned out to sub units.

To maintain secrecy and to foster a sense of belonging units adopted titles, sometimes slogans such as 'Death to the Fascist Occupiers' or the names of Soviet/Russian heroes, 'In the name of Lenin' or similar. Names that advertised a location were avoided for security reasons. Despite being called 'brigade' or 'company', few units ever met any normal headcount and frequently fell well below such norms. Consequently a brigade with two or three battalions could number no more than 200–300 combatants. However, the structure was in place for expansion, although replacing casualties in a tight-knit partisan section could be problematic and newcomers would have to prove their worth by their deeds.

Furthermore they would have to learn the little ways and traditions that such groups developed. Official and unofficial probationary periods were accepted parts of life for any would-be member of a partisan unit at any level. Ranks were as per the army for officers but NCOs as such do not appear to have existed; chain of command seems to have depended on seniority and experience. However, woe betide the formation that did not have a designated *Politruk*: these Moscow deemed as indispensable to ensure the unit's reliability and curb any 'deviationist' tendencies. The usual form of address was traditionally Russian, name and patronymic, with a rank being substituted for officers unless the situation and relationship merited otherwise.

Possibly one of the 'Winners' female radio operators, a Spanish communist Africa de las Heras, dressed in the unit's paratrooper overall tucked into boots with her hair cut short. (Courtesy of the Central Museum of the Armed Forces Moscow via www.stavka.org.uk)

APPEARANCE

Clearly it is essential that partisans, wherever they are operating, blend in with the local population in terms of what they wear and how they wear it, their hairstyle, their footwear, their speech and their general manner of conducting themselves. Tsessarsky and others commented that everywhere they went they were referred to as 'Muscovites' simply because of their accents. Happily it was too subtle a difference for the vast majority of the occupation forces to pick up on. Pre-*Barbarossa* experience had taught the NKVD the importance of attention to detail and this was imbued into their recruits as the following example shows. During 1940, 'The security service of the Ukrainian nationalists quickly traced some of the safe houses of the Ukrainian NKVD in Lvov. Their method was simple: they organized a surveillance post near the NKVD HQ and followed every man coming out in civilian clothes wearing high boots, the normal gear of military dress. Ukrainian *Chekists* covered their uniforms with coats but forgot to change their boots... In western Ukraine everyone other than the military wore short boots.'

A sailor turned partisan. His cap tally identifies him as a member of the ship *Zealous*. This peakless cap was known as a *beskozirka*. Under his outer garments he is probably wearing the black and white hooped undershirt, *telniashka*. If stripped to this it signified no retreat, no surrender. (Courtesy of the Central Museum of the Armed Forces Moscow via www.stavka.org.uk)

When recruits joined OMSBON during 1941 they were issued with standard NKVD uniforms without badges of rank or branch of service indicators such as collar flashes. This consisted of a tunic, the model 1936 *gymnastiorka* – a pull-over tunic with a stand and fall collar, jodhpur style breeches known as *sharovari* and a *pilotka* side cap, generally worn at a

Part of Kovpak's unit during the summer of 1943. Several German police tunics are in evidence as are various items of Red Army kit. In the main the dress is typically civilian. The jackets and trousers were generally drab in colour as were the caps. One of the central figures is wearing a *shlem* or *budionovka*, as issued to the Red Army from 1920 into the 1930s. (From the fonds of the RGAKFD, Kranogorsk via www.stavka.org.uk)

rakish angle over the right eye, with a red enamel star to the front. These items were khaki drab, the shade of which depended on the number of times it had been laundered, ranging from dark to light olive verging on white. Tunic and breeches were issued in wool for the winter and cotton for the summer. Footwear was, in many cases, a matter of luck. Two of Tsessarsky's comrades had difficulties: one had feet too large, the other too small; consequently they both wore sports shoes. Black leather knee boots shod everyone else with foot cloths, *portyanki*, replacing socks. During 1941 priority was given to the front-line troops and OMSBON had to wait for items to appear when available. Officers came equipped with uniforms as they were all pre-war regulars, and wore their branch of service dress that was NKVD frontier guard issue. This comprised a button-up tunic – the *kitel*, breeches of better cut and finer cloth with four pockets on the tunic and a peaked cap – the *furashka*. The cap was medium green, with a black band piped at the top in crimson, as was the crown. Breeches were dark blue with a red seam stripe that tucked into black knee boots. Badges of rank were worn on collar and cuffs until 1943 when shoulder boards, *pogoni*, were reintroduced. Other ranks merely wore a simple brown leather belt, officers a Sam Browne belt. Winter wear was not issued until the unit was mobilized to provide security in and around Moscow from mid-October 1941 and then not everyone received a full set due to shortages. The clothing should have included a padded tunic – *telogreika*, padded *sharovari* and a fur-lined, wool cap. This ensemble would be worn over the winter tunic and breeches. The winter greatcoat – *shuba*, was sheepskin with the wool inside and the natural hide exposed. All Russian troops padded themselves as much as possible during the winter and on occasion looked grotesquely overweight; heat retention was the prime concern. Steel helmets of either the M1936 or M1939 versions, or even the older type based on the French Adrian of 1916, were issued as available. The unit's women, radio operators or medical assistants, were issued with the standard tunic but were expected to wear a khaki skirt and beret. Male attire was usually adapted in the field.

Any tailoring required to repair clothing was done by comrades with the requisite skills. As was common in the Russian military, badges and later medals were worn displayed. Many of the recruits had achieved marksmanship, riding and parachuting distinctions through the auspices of OSOAVIAKhIM which they were allowed to wear as long as they did not give away the wearer's position to the enemy. OMSBOM members had no distinguishing marks on their uniforms as they were a secret unit and therefore wore nothing to draw attention to themselves. When they were dispatched behind enemy lines they continued to dress as ordinary Red Army men. In the case of the 'Winners' however, many of the photographs of them in the field show them dressed in

A rather languid member of Kovpak's unit strikes a pose for the camera. The rakishly worn straw-hat contrasts with the drab rain cape, *plashch-palatka*, and light summer jacket over an open *gymnastiorka*. (From the fonds of the RGAKFD, Kranogorsk via www.stavka.org.uk)

paratroopers' one-piece coveralls. Certainly many of the 'Winners' had been parachuted or airlifted into position and this was obviously a practical garment to wear. The design dated from 1933 and was khaki drab with a fly front concealing buttons, two breast pockets and two large patch pockets on the thigh. Insignia does not seem to have been worn with this item. Replacement uniforms were flown in during their campaign.

Inevitably they scavenged clothes and equipment from their enemies. Of particular value were German security forces uniforms or those uniforms worn by collaborationist units such as the Ost Battalions raised from POWs

Typical partisans in their everyday clothes. It was men such as these who made up the bulk of the partisans' strength. Dressed in cloth caps, jackets, trousers and boots there is little attempt at uniformity. They appear to have rain capes wrapped around their chests. (Courtesy of the Central Museum of the Armed Forces Moscow via www.stavka.org.uk)

or deserters. Boris Chorny recalled dressing in police uniforms when passing through villages of indeterminate loyalty in western Ukraine. Nikolai Kuznetsov, an NKVD agent who specialized in intelligence-gathering by dressing as a German officer, was particularly adept in this role, spending weeks at a time in disguise when the slightest slip could have cost him his life.

For the *Okruzhentsy* it was unlikely that they had much more than the clothes they stood up in: boots, *gymnastiorka*, *sharovari* and *pilotka* or helmet. On joining a partisan unit they tended to retain as much of a military appearance as possible to confirm their status as 'real soldiers'.

In the civilian and Party formations dress was not generally regulated or uniform. However, some units took to wearing a piece of red cloth as a field recognition sign, as had been the style of the impromptu Red Guards during the revolutionary period. This was worn as a brassard or on headgear, particularly the winter fur hats. German tunics were often worn to fool the security forces and local populace. Indeed when the 'Glorious' partisan group was moving from Ukraine to Belarus it was necessary to march in daylight. A German aircraft passed overhead but did not open fire. 'Perhaps it took us for its own. On one of our carts we prudently displayed a large flag with the swastika. A significant proportion of our men wore German uniform.' The same unit used German overalls to approach a position fooling the enemy into holding their fire until it was too late.

 RUSSIAN WEAPONS

For obvious reasons partisans used Soviet equipment. The weapons were available in quantity, they were familiar and they were easy to maintain in primitive workshops.

1a–1b Standard-issue Mosin-Nagant M1891/30 7.62mm rifles. 1a has its canvas/webbing sling and an additional 3.5 PU telescopic sight.

1c Tokarev SVT 40 automatic rifle.

1d Mosin-Nagant 7.62mm carbine.

2a PPD-40 sub-machine gun.

2b PPSh-41 with the 35-round box magazine.

2c PPD-43 with 'banana' magazine.

3a DT 7.62mm Tank machine gun. These were designed with dismounted action in mind, hence the detachable bipod. The stock is ratcheted to allow for adjustment and the magazine held 60 rounds.

3b DP 7.62mm 'record player' machine gun with folded bipod.

4a Pressed metal ammunition box for record player magazines.

4b Canvas pouch for PPSh/D magazines. It was attached to a belt by two loops.

5a M1933 Tokarev pistol; there were several series of these handguns made that varied slightly. Its holster is to rear.

5b M1895 Nagant revolver with holster to rear.

6a Bayonet for an SVT 50 with its sheath.

6b Hunting knife and decorated sheath.

6c Hunting knife with leather scabbard

7a RPG-40 anti-tank grenade

7b RGD-33 blast grenade with fragmentation sheath.

7c F1 fragmentation grenade

8a Red Army cartridge pouch

8b SVT-40 ammunition pouch

The central figure is a former POW who is wearing a Red Army shirt and *pilotka* side cap, a civilian jacket with German M1940 riding breeches with leather crotch reinforcement. He is armed with the PPSh-41 and based on a member of Kovpak's unit. The partisan medal next to him was issued from 1943 onwards and came in two classes, first and second. The second class was bronze with a blue stripe, the first silver with a red stripe.

1a 1b 1c 1d 2a 2b 2c 3a 3b

8a

8b

7a 7b 7c

6a 6b 6c

4a

4b

5a

5b

П. Карашук
2013

When S. V. Rudnev's group merged with Kovpak's force, his men, imitating Rudnev himself, all sported moustaches. Rudnev's was described as a 'jet black, large bushy growth that was always carefully brushed'. His men paid equal attention to their facial hair to the point where they were often waxed, even sculpted. Rudnev was also fastidious about his clothes, 'his white tunic and collar, as usual impeccably clean'. Generally the united force wore civilian clothing or items of Red Army uniform. Particularly valued were the Axis-issue rain capes that could be assembled into small tents.

The contrast between the Medvedev and Kovpak units was underlined by Boris Chorny who was detailed to act as a guide for Kovpak. One of Kovpak's men described the 'Winners' in this manner: 'you aren't a partisan platoon but a school for noble girls'. The remark was aimed at the 'Winners' comparatively fastidious attitude to their clothing, neat hair and clean-shaven faces.

EQUIPMENT

A partisan scout, warmly clad in his army issue two-piece snowsuit, keeps watch. Layering of clothing was essential to retain heat, particularly in situations where immobility was vital. On his feet he appears to have the *valenki* pressed felt boots, which were ideal in these conditions but decomposed when wet. (Courtesy of the Central Museum of the Armed Forces Moscow via www.stavka.org.uk)

The Russian military has always been noted for its equipment's ease of construction, operation and maintenance. Weapons were simply engineered with a minimum of parts to clean and repair to maximize 'soldier proofing'.

Whenever the regime replaced the infantry rifle a significant percentage was always sold off to private individuals. Therefore it was not uncommon to find Berdan rifles from the 1870s working just as well in 1941 in the hands of huntsmen. During the chaos of the Central Powers' withdrawal from Russia in 1918–19 and the Russian Civil War of 1917–21 hundreds of thousands of guns of all types had been acquired by the peasantry as well as the authorities. Ammunition was also plentiful as vast quantities had just been abandoned. Consequently the Mauser Model 1898, the Mannlicher Model 1895 and the Mosin-Nagant Model 1891 were common, as were the skills required to maintain them. Indeed, although the Mosin-Nagant had received minimal upgrades during the 1920s resulting in the model 1891/1930, it was basically the same weapon and remained the standard infantry rifle throughout the war and beyond.

When Rudnev's men joined Kovpak's it was noted that they brought '57 men, 49 rifles of different systems, six carbines and a machine gun'. The machine gun was doubtless the Russian Model 1910 maxim, with shield and two-wheeled carriage familiar from World War I. However, what the combined force lacked in standardized firepower they made up for in mines and improvised explosive devices. As it fell back the Red Army laid thousands of mines that had subsequently been abandoned. The partisans harvested dozens and several were laid on a nearby road where they disabled a German lorry resulting in the acquisition of 10,000 rounds of small arms ammunition. The Red Army commonly deployed three types of mine: the POMZ, a stake-mounted anti-personnel mine activated by tripwire; the PMD-6 and PMD-7, both anti-personnel mines that were pressure-detonated with wooden cases; the TM-35 was a rectangular, metal-cased, anti-tank mine containing up to 2.8kg of TNT. Detonated by pressure it could also incorporate anti-handling devices, which endangered anyone tampering with it. These mines were ideal for creating defensive zones around partisan camps and, if carefully mapped, could be easily retrieved.

Although at first grateful for any weapon, the range of such available began to expand as the partisans took equipment from their enemies and began to receive supplies by air. The preferred light machine gun rapidly became the DP Model 1928 that used standard 7.62mm rifle ammunition loaded via a flat pan magazine which gave rise to its nickname – the record player. At roughly 10kg loaded it was easily portable and remarkably resistant to dust and dirt. Its major drawback was that it was only capable of automatic (continuous) fire. The Maxim's replacement heavy machine gun, the DShK Model 1938, was a more complex weapon than its predecessor and did not prove popular, as it was difficult to maintain.

Captured, in Russian parlance 'trophy', equipment was widely used. Commonly found was the German light machine gun MG Model 1934. Twice as heavy as the 'record player' it was also engineered to a much higher standard, thus proving difficult to maintain. It also jammed when dusty, damp or dirty; therefore it required a crew well versed in its idiosyncrasies to keep it in action. The more robust MG Model 1942 was, however, rarer but highly rated by those partisans who used it. Above all other firearms the Soviet PPD and PPSh sub-machine guns were by far the most popular for simplicity, firepower and reliability. Officers usually carried side arms although many partisans obtained them. The most widespread was the Nagant Model 1895

Nikolai Ivanovich Kuznetsov in German officer's uniform. In the role of Lt. Paul Seibert, an officer of Prussian descent, on active service with Infanterie-Regiment 230 (destroyed at Stalingrad) from August 1940 and a holder of the Iron Cross 1st class. He is wearing a modified M1940 other ranks tunic, breeches and leather reinforced felt boots. His headgear is a field grey cloth cap lined with rabbit fur. (From the fonds of the RGAKFD, Kranogorsk via www.stavka.org.uk)

Red Army men who escaped from or avoided captivity were grateful to get away with their lives. Although appearance was the least of their worries they did try to maintain a sense of identity. (Nik Cornish@ www.stavka.org.uk)

revolver that carried seven rounds of 7.62mm ammunition. A close second to this was the Tokarev Model 1933, similar in appearance to the Colt model 1911. A self-loading piece that fired a 7.62mm round, it was highly regarded for its 'stopping power' if not for its accuracy. Again both were easy to look after in the field. Cold steel was a matter of personal choice, often based on the capacity of the individual to actually use it in close combat. Shortened, sharpened bayonets were popular as they provided a firm grip: hunting knives were also in widespread use.

Radios were not common in the USSR. Party offices usually had one, as did the occasional school, but their use was heavily regulated, limited to receiving broadcasts from the capital – the Voice of Moscow. When the security forces arrived radios were confiscated to limit the population's access to news from anywhere other than Axis sources. During late 1941 the Germans spread the rumour that Moscow had fallen and the Red Army was falling back to the Ural Mountains. A local teacher, who had hidden a radio, approached Kovpak offering it to him: the gift was received with open arms. As the group possessed a generator, taken from a German convoy, it was a

B **AXIS WEAPONS**

Captured weapons formed a large percentage of partisan units' arsenals.
1   A selection of homemade belt buckles with appliqué red stars to denote their new owners.
2   The German MG34 was delicate weapon. Twice as heavy as the 'record player' it was engineered to a much higher standard thus proving difficult to maintain. It also jammed when dusty, damp or dirty therefore it required a crew well versed in its idiosyncrasies to keep it in action.
3   A Czech-made ZB-30 light machine gun. With a calibre of 7.92mm it was fed by a 30-round box magazine. It was widely used by German security and second-line units.
4   Another German weapon, the MG08/15 with its magazine below. A vintage weapon dating from 1915, large numbers were captured by the partisans from German security forces. It was water cooled and belt fed. Weighing in at 18kg it was heavier and more unwieldy than the 'record player'
5a   Leather pouch for MP40 magazines.
5b   Leather magazine pouch for an MP34. The strip magazine was attached to the left side of the gun and held 32 rounds.
5c   Canvas pouch for MP40 magazines.
6   Swiss/Austrian-made Steyr-Solothurn MP34, widely issued to German police and security formations.
7   German MP40 sub-machine gun with its stock folded. A highly prized trophy weapon which was light and highly effective as well as easy to maintain.
8   MP41 with wooden stock. These were issued to SS and police units.
9a   Mauser C96 with wooden stock/holster. A popular weapon in a variety of models it was highly prized.
9b   A Luger PO8, the standard German sidearm. It was accurate and reliable with an eight-round capacity.
9c   The Walther PP (Polizei Pistole) was a 7.65mm piece with an eight-round detachable magazine lodged in the handle.
9d   Another Walther, the semi-automatic P38 was designed to replace the more expensive Luger.
10a   Luger holster.
10b   Luger holster (variant).
10c   Walther P38 holster.
10d   Walther PP holster.
The figure represents a partisan equipped exclusively with captured items. He is holding an M1934 98k rifle. In his waist belt is a German M1924 stick grenade, the 6x30 binoculars and ammunition pouches are standard German issue. His dress is typical of that worn in the countryside in the recruitment area of A. F. Fedorov's units that operated in Ukraine and Belarus.

1a 1b

1c 1d

2

3

4

5b 5c 5a

6

7

8

9a 9b

9c

9d

10a 10b 10c 10d

simple matter to power the radio. From this the unit was able to write down the news bulletins from Moscow. These would be hand-copied and distributed to neighbouring villages. The copies were further copied and thus news spread around the district. Other partisan groups used this method so that even though transmitters were rare receivers could be found. This essential service was expanded upon during 1942 when several partisan units obtained simple printing presses, often from Moscow and occasionally by 'liberating' them, as Kovpak's men did, and began to print newssheets. Consequently paper and ink entered the 'shopping lists' sent to Moscow. The fillip news from the 'Great Land' provided to morale was incalculable as was the support it gave to reinforcing the Soviet regime's authority in the 'Temporarily Occupied Territories'.

As 1942 began it became clear that the return of the Red Army was not imminent and the occupation would continue with increasing severity. Therefore establishing wireless communication with Moscow and the Red Army was vital. Although letters had been passed across the front line, in the confusion of the time Moscow was unaware of the situation behind enemy lines and often deeply suspicious of those who claimed to be partisans due to the unexpectedly high level of collaboration. Consequently Moscow was not prepared to provide such luxuries as radios to units that might well be bogus. Happily for Kovpak his formation was recognized and during April 1942 three radio operators plus their equipment were successfully parachuted in and regular communications established with the capital.

At the end of May the Central HQ of the Partisan Movement was established in Moscow to co-ordinate and oversee the movement other than NKVD units. During the summer of 1942 when radio and other communications had been established partisan leaders were summoned to Moscow. This operation was undertaken by air from landing strips prepared by the partisans at pre-arranged sites. The aircraft employed was fondly known to the partisans as the 'Douglas' or the 'heavenly slug'. It was a licence-built version of the DC-3, the LI-2, which was capable of using rough, improvised runways. The LI-2 could carry 24 passengers or 14 stretcher cases and would be used throughout the war in specially allocated partisan support flights. It was from these aircraft that OMSBON personnel were usually dropped into action. Defence was provided by a dorsal turret mounting a 7.62mm ShKAS machine gun. They were also used to transport munitions and all manner of supplies as their undercarriage easily adapted to skis so that winter weather was not too problematic. For shorter hops U-2 or PO-2 biplanes with their short take-off and landing capabilities were ideal.

As well as giving Stalin an opportunity to appraise the more significant partisan leaders, the visit to Moscow led to Kovpak's formation being given a mission by the 'Boss' as the leader of the USSR was known. Kovpak provided Stalin with an oral list of equipment his unit required: 'Most of all what we need [are] rifles, machine guns, anti-tank guns'. According to the memoirs of one of his staff, everyone 'knew Kovpak was addicted to "the Gods of War" [artillery]'. Boots were also included for, despite having a tailoring facility, leather was in short supply. Shortly after Kovpak returned to his base the promised supplies and more, including medicines, uniforms and propaganda materials, arrived. The latter was a vital element of the partisans' equipment as an important, sometimes overlooked aspect of their work was the re-establishment of Soviet authority, the re-enforcement of the

Dressed in a variety of outfits, including a modified German police jacket (left), this group of partisans typifies the appearance of those groups that formed in the countryside. The female medical orderly is carrying a canvas equipment bag marked with a red cross. (Courtesy of the Central Museum of the Armed Forces Moscow via www.stavka.org.uk)

concept of a Soviet victory and the return of Communism. The partisans were viewed by Moscow as their representatives in the occupied lands.

To move men and equipment on a mission such as that of Kovpak or the 'Winners' it was essential that transport be procured. All across the countryside the standard vehicle was the *panje* wagon. With high, thin wheels and a boat-like body it was ideally suited to negotiate the snow and mud that caused such disruption to the supply units of the invaders. Drawn by the hardy breeds of horse that centuries of harsh conditions had inured to the lack of food and continual hard work, the wagons and sledges proved ideal for terrain where even the toughest motor vehicle would find it hard to cope. *Panje* wagons were the backbone of the partisan logistics chain. Hired or borrowed in one village they would be replaced in another. Boris Chorny recalled that the 'Winners' paid for such items in *Reichsmarks*, which provoked the locals to ask, 'Why do you give us German money?' 'So you can use it,' was the reply; it cost the Soviets nothing as the cash was often forged in Moscow. The draught animals were perfectly capable of foraging in snow up to a metre deep and finding sufficient nourishment to keep them healthy. The wagons and sledges were solidly built, easy to maintain and simple to harness; furthermore they were generally driven by experienced hands who were well aware of their capabilities. They were true all-terrain vehicles that were capable of carrying up to eight men. During the Carpathian Raid of 1943 Kovpak's baggage train consisted of over 300 *panje* wagons. This meant a probable 500–600 horses to feed and care for. During the Russian Civil War and supposedly invented by the Ukrainian anarchists, the *tachanka* – a farmer's carriage, had been adapted as a machine-gun transport doubling as a firing platform mounting a rear-facing Maxim machine gun. More solidly built than the *panje* wagon, these appear to have seen occasional use with partisan formations. However, it was more usual to see the weapon dismounted. Equally rare was the use of motor vehicles as partisan warfare was essentially highly mobile and the limitations placed on movement and concealment by the use of trucks would have invalidated any gains.

During the winter skis and snowshoes were also vital for rapid movement by individuals. As with all personal equipment the individual partisan was responsible for day-to-day maintenance. This was particularly true for specialists such as radio operators, machine-gunners, and mortar and artillery crews.

Alongside the weapons, the cash, the propaganda material, the clothing and the more martial equipment fruit also featured. Having destroyed several bridges during the winter of 1942 Kovpak's men ran out of explosives. They decided to improvise and hung several large pumpkins from the last bridge where they would be in clear sight. German engineers spotted them immediately and 'for more than two weeks racked their brains trying to unravel the hidden mechanism in the pumpkins'. Eventually the decoys rotted, however, during that time the bridge had been unusable.

CONDITIONS OF SERVICE

Food preparation and storage was vital. Partisan units were expected to live off of the land. Supplies were bought from locals or 'liberated' from the enemy. Hunting and fishing supplemented what could be obtained from elsewhere. Salt was an incredibly precious commodity. (Courtesy of the Central Museum of the Armed Forces Moscow via www.stavka.org.uk)

There is no simple rule of thumb to describe the partisans' conditions of service certainly in the amateur formations. The civilian groups organized by the Party were, theoretically, drawn from volunteers who were allowed to elect their own officers who would in their turn 'take guidance from the HQ staff composed of members of the executive committees of the regional, district and village Soviets (councils)'. Kovpak remembered 'not just the city dweller but also the farmers of the surrounding villages and hamlets are afraid to get lost in this maze of forest roads and trails'. Consequently getting used to the environment in which they would live and operate was a major factor during the early days. Indeed fear of discovery before the group coalesced into a fighting unit provoked problems. This came to a head when experimenting with mines. Some of the group grumbled that the sound of the explosions would attract the attention of the Germans. Therefore Kovpak assembled the men and pointed out that 'if anyone came to the forest, hoping to sit quietly [or] to collect mushrooms and nuts it is better they go'. No reference was made to anyone leaving. In part this wait and see mentality was due to the fact that many 'fair weather' partisans anticipated the speedy return of the Red Army and had joined up simply to gain post-war kudos with the Soviet regime. Antipathy towards what were disparagingly referred to later as 'newly minted partisans' was widespread and it was only when the dangers of the situation became crystal clear that such 'wannabes' slunk quietly away to live with the opprobrium that their actions generated when liberation came.

Kovpak's small force spent its time building a large, concealed dugout in which to live while simultaneously laying down the basis of the unit's organizational and command structure.

Scavenging was generally the way in which most rural partisans gathered their first weapons. The machine gun in the middle is an Austrian-made Schwarzlose Model 1907/12 that was issued to German and Hungarian security forces. A shield from a Russian Maxim has been added. It was another simple, robust design ideally suited to partisan use. The mortar tubes and stands appear to be Soviet 107mm Model 1938 types backed with Mosin-Nagant rifles. (Courtesy of the Central Museum of the Armed Forces Moscow via www.stavka.org.uk)

When the first group of Red Army stragglers arrived they formed a separate section and when Rudnev's force amalgamated he became the Political Commissar sharing overall responsibility with Kovpak and bringing the formation in line with Soviet military practice.

Routines were established as men became accustomed to cleaning weapons, mounting patrols, standing guard, gathering and preparing food, getting to know their new comrades and the unfamiliar paths of the forest. Drilling and weapons training were carried out under the eyes of veterans or newly arrived soldiers. As the front line had moved eastwards and the area was not yet occupied it was still possible to venture into the local population centres for food and other necessaries. However, when the Germans launched their first attack it was decided to move deeper into the forest. To ease food supply the unit split into eight sections but as the autumn turned to winter and the local security forces tightened their grip over the local population's movements it was vital to make plans for surviving the winter. Storage facilities were dug for food and fuel laid in. No one was exempt from these duties unless otherwise occupied; consequently there was little or no opportunity for relaxation. Concerns about partisans' families living in occupied areas began to sap morale. It was therefore decided that the entire situation needed formalizing to give an overarching sense of purpose to why they were away from hearth and home. Consequently the leadership drew up an oath of allegiance to bind the group together, the wording of which reads as follows: 'As a guerrilla I swear before all the Soviet people, the Party and the government that I will fight for the liberation of my country from the yoke of Fascism to the complete destruction of it.'

Effectively a précis of the Red Army oath, each man repeated the text in front of his comrades and then signed or made his mark on the document. This was carried out in descending order of rank. Other areas adopted similar oaths that were approved by their local Party organization and doubtless Moscow as well.

This man is carrying the standard-issue Red Army Mosin-Nagant Model 1891/307.62mm calibre. Ammunition for the five-round magazine is carried in the canvas bandoliers worn across the chest. It was designed for a socket bayonet attachment, which the partisans generally used as a separate weapon as it extended the rifle's length rendering it unwieldy in woody areas. (Courtesy of the Central Museum of the Armed Forces Moscow via www.stavka.org.uk)

Some of the families judged to be at risk were spirited away to the forest, but as the winter of 1941–42 was so harsh little or no combat took place as both sides were more concerned about surviving in relative comfort. The partisans passed the time in training, sleeping and improving their shelter. For many other groups this period marked their demise. It has been estimated that over 80 per cent of those partisans that Moscow was aware of either died or melted back into the population during this season. Kovpak's unit was one of the rare exceptions. With the worst of the winter over it was decided to celebrate Red Army Day on 23 February 1942 to reinforce the message of faith in ultimate victory. Representatives of all the partisan formations that could be contacted gathered in a remote village where a parade was to be held. When the speechifying and marching had ended, the celebrations were concluded with music from the partisan band which included four accordions and a violinist, and a period of emotional silence when the assembly listened to Moscow radio and a speech by Stalin that raised morale dramatically when he announced 'Long live the men and women guerrillas', as well as declaring that Moscow was safe due to the Red Army's counter offensive.

As some partisans had medical experience local civilians began to come to them for advice on treatment and, in the absence of pharmaceuticals, natural medicines. Typhus was particularly worrying due to the conditions in which the partisans lived, as their quarters were cramped and often overcrowded bunkers. Poor diet contributed to cases of scurvy. Both diseases were fought by a combination of hygiene and discipline; people were ordered to bathe at regular intervals and observe a of careful, ration-controlled diet. When conditions and security permitted partisan medics would tour the area lecturing the people on health and hygiene as well as distributing news and information from Moscow and collecting foodstuffs. As the occupation policies of the Germans became clearer and their obvious disinterest in the well being of their new subjects more blatant the partisans stepped in to fill the void. While there was no serious fighting going on the partisans were very active in restoring a semblance of the old Soviet regime in what became known as Partisan *krais*. Several such areas slowly came into being behind German lines, particularly around Bryansk and in the neighbouring forests where few security troops dared venture. In the *krai* the partisans maintained Soviet law, encouraged its culture, supported educational facilities and defied the enemy. These islands of Soviet 'normality' served as rallying points for those who came to hear of them and they continued to develop and grow throughout 1942. The partisans in these areas subsumed the duties of local government but subject to martial law. By absorbing established communities, however, there were partisan groups that ruled their little fiefdoms much as warlords of the Middle Ages, abusing their power and behaving in such a manner that their behaviour was in part the reason for Stalin summoning the leaders to a conference during the spring of 1942. This meeting with the 'amateurs' in the field combined with the establishment of the Central HQ of the Partisan Movement put the partisans firmly under Moscow's control,

reducing the possibility of any deviation from the Party line to the margins. Partisan leaders were given military rank and the powers and responsibilities that went with such status. From mid-1942 the partisan was essentially a Red Army soldier subject to the discipline of that organization and with all the responsibilities that it entailed.

This had been the case for OMSBON recruits from the beginning. Their conditions of service were simply outlined and they accepted from the start that they were soldiers. Having accustomed themselves to a more regimented way of life during their pre-deployment training and while undertaking defensive and security duties during the winter of 1941–42 in and around Moscow they were to undergo further guerrilla training before being sent behind enemy lines. Once inserted 'everyday life was fighting' as Boris Chorny recalled. One member of the 'Winners' was executed for looting, this onerous duty being carried out by the unit's Commissar. This event took place in western Ukraine where the population was less Russophile in its loyalties and the partisans were at pains to demonstrate the good behaviour of 'Muscovites'. To treat these people badly would make life extremely dangerous for Medvedev's force consequently one life lost was regarded as a cheap price for the unit's survival. If the execution achieved nothing else it kept potential 'hostiles' neutral.

Despite Chorny's earlier comment the 'Winners' did have quiet moments to fill. One of Tsessarsky's colleagues who had been a student of philosophy and literature before joining OMSBON was sent to observe German military traffic on a stretch of road for two days. In between taking notes he wrote a biography of the Shakespearean character Yorick; the notes he made were subsequently published posthumously. Along with others Tsessarsky took part in a 'partisan' version of Hamlet, substituting modern weapons for those of the period, around the campfire to amuse their comrades. Other former students of various disciplines often engaged in debates and lectures on their particular speciality. Tsessarsky, diplomatically, refrained from passing judgement on how well these were received.

Casualty evacuation by air was rare in comparison with the number of wounded simply carried from place to place. Four men are carrying this casualty lying on a blanket slung between two Birch branches. (From the fonds of the RGAKFD, Kranogorsk via www.stavka.org.uk)

Belarusian partisans with an impressive array of firepower. The left-hand man is carrying a PPD-40 with a 71-round drum magazine. A pre-war weapon, manufacture of which was abandoned in favour of the weapons seen with the second, third and fifth figures from the left – the ubiquitous PPSH-41. It was crude, reliable and effective and a trophy prized by the Germans for its simplicity. The man on the right has a PPS-42/43. With a 'banana' magazine that held 35 rounds it was the equal in all respects of the PPSh. (Courtesy of the Central Museum of the Armed Forces Moscow via www.stavka.org.uk)

The 'Winners', in common with other groups, were of mixed gender. During their time on active service from 1942–44 eight weddings took place in Tsessarsky's unit alone. The couple had to first obtain Medvedev's permission as Commander then he and the Commissar performed the ceremony according to Soviet law. The couple were joined in matrimony, with the whole force looking on. A special fruit pie was baked and then eaten.

COMMUNICATIONS APPARATUS

The availability of communications systems was, in the early months of the partisan movement, severely limited. The problem was further compounded by the lack of operators and technical support, if a component was broken then the radio became useless. Nor was there any central body through or with which to communicate. One of the first tasks of the Central Headquarters of the Partisan Movement was to establish radio communications with the dozens of different units. A training school for radio operators had been established which graduated the majority of the operatives sent to join the partisan units. The first intake consisted of part trained, via OSOAVIAKhIM, Komsomol members. The first course began in February 1942.

1. This is the standard issue radio station North (*Sever* in Russian). Produced in Leningrad and Moscow it was originally known as the Omega. The canvas bag to rear carries the BA-80 batteries. A robust piece of kit, battery and station it weighed 14kg and had a range of 500km. It was originally designed for use by troops on the Northern Front hence the name. However, its relatively short range made it less useful in areas such as Ukraine.

2. The radio station RPO-4 was used by units in Ukraine due to its range. RPO means Radio Partisan Group. This set could be powered manually but the process was very noisy.

3. Radio station Squirrel (*Belka* in Russian) was a fragile piece of kit.

4. This radio station, the RBM-1, was rare. It weighed 11.5kg excluding batteries. Introduced in 1942 it was being replaced less than a year later. Naturally this was not often the case for partisan units that were simply pleased to have any radio equipment.

5. Radio station 'Partisan'. As its name implies a station designed specifically for partisan units, it is similar to the RPO-4.

6. A radio operator making a transmission on her North equipment. Sending unencrypted messages was strictly forbidden and most operators memorised their codes and call signs. Operators were not generally included when a unit undertook a combat mission as their specialist skills were too difficult to replace. Furthermore their knowledge of codes, communications systems and methodology made them highly valued targets for the anti-partisan forces. If the batteries were carried in a separate container the resulting wire connection impeded speedy relocation.

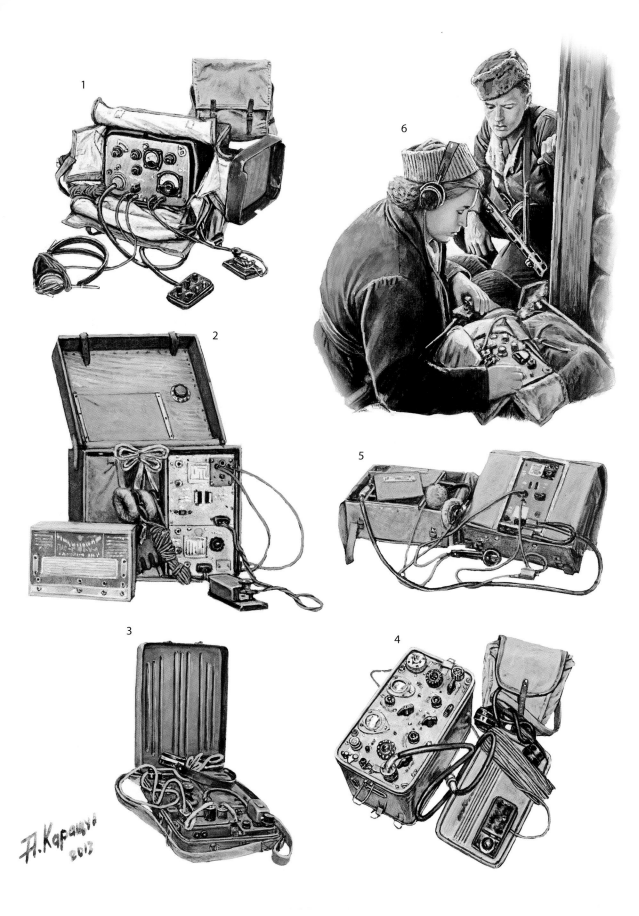

This young partisan shows off four hand grenades. To the right is an RGD-33 without the fragmentation sleeve, to the left the RPG-40. Behind each is a Model 1914 Russian stick grenade. The Soviet F1 was widely issued. (Courtesy of the Central Museum of the Armed Forces Moscow via www.stavka.org.uk)

Two of the brides were radio operators, generally a female preserve. Unfortunately one marriage ended in divorce. However, extra-marital relations were strictly forbidden as was rape, the latter punishable by death. The 'Winners', according to Tsessarsky, harboured no homosexuals – it was 'impossible, homosexuality was illegal in the USSR'. Nor were any abortions performed, as that too was illegal under Soviet law. Boris Chorny remembered giving one pair of newly-weds a blanket as a present and said 'love is love, women got pregnant'; he implied that Medvedev, on such occasions, consulted with the medical staff as to what course of action to take.

For Medvedev's self-confessed 'city boys' rural life was something of a shock. Negotiating with farmers to buy food, animal husbandry and shelter building had all been part of the training programme, putting them into practice for real was another matter. So too was the reality of dealing with refugees or recruits who sought sanctuary with the partisans, be they Jews fleeing from the ghettoes, Axis deserters or patriotic locals who wished to do their duty. Sadly anti-Semitism was widespread and deeply ingrained amongst many Belarusian and Ukrainian partisan groups which resulted in the establishment of purely Jewish partisan formations such as that led by the Bielski brothers immortalized in the film *Defiance*. When the 'Winners' were approached by a group of Jewish refugees they provided them with food and shelter. Having discussed the matter with Medvedev, Chorny (himself a Jew) recalled Medvedev saying, 'We can't feed them all. This is what I'll do, give them paratrooper smocks, one or two rifles and send them to Belarus – it's quieter there.' Chorny was tasked with leading them to the right track; however, the group broke up within days preferring to return to their previous hideouts. A small number of younger Jews remained with the 'Winners' as combatants.

Interestingly one of Kovpak's men commented that once they were given their first mission by Moscow he anticipated 'the first few days to be filled with raids, fights and mass heroism'. He was rather deflated that all they seemed to do was march 'throughout the night and at dawn park in the forest'. However, when one of Kovpak's scouting parties discovered a cache of alcohol they, in the absence of senior officers, proceeded to get drunk. The offenders were gently disciplined, but it was obvious to the leadership that their men needed action. The artillery was brought up and a police post in a nearby village attacked. This small, successful action 'blooded' some of the more hot-headed partisans, giving them a more realistic idea of what war was all about – real bullets causing real casualties. Following that episode drinking whilst on or off duty without permission was punished severely. Medvedev would not allow foul language in his unit and the punishment for this was the unpopular cookhouse chore of grinding cereals to make bread. However, by punishing small offences he achieved a high level of discipline that span off onto the satellite units formed under the 'Winners' umbrella.

ON CAMPAIGN

Life under canvas when training during the summer of 1941 did little to prepare the members of OMSBON for the rigours of campaign life. Their first deployment was as part of the forces deployed to defend Moscow from mid-October 1941. Given the uncertainty and near-panic generated by the speed of the German advance on the capital, trustworthy units such as those of the NKVD, no matter how inexperienced, were tasked with defending the city centre where lay the nerve centre and symbol of Communist rule – the Kremlin. OMSBON units were spread from the Kremlin to the Belarus railway station and, ominously, the Vagankovsky cemetery. For many of the men and women their homes were just down the road from where they were dug in. As one commented, 'the war came straight to our house'. As the Red Army successfully held the city few of the OSMBON troops saw action. One that did was Albert Tsessarsky. He and his platoon were defending a position south-west of the capital near Mozhaisk on the Moskva River. Here they shot at a German machine-gun post that was taking pot shots at refugees who were trying to cross the frozen river. Witnessing this sort of behaviour at first hand strengthened their resolve to fight on and their desire for revenge; war was no longer a theoretical exercise. When the order to counterattack was issued on 5 December 1941, Tsessarsky and his comrades were elated. 'I'm not an evil man but when I saw dead Germans, one with a bra on his head, I had a feeling of satisfaction.'

Shortly after this the OMSBON were replaced by regular troops and Tsessarsky was allocated to Medvedev's command where his first duty was to 'sort out the healthiest men'. A total of 480 volunteers came forward from OMSBON's ranks but Medvedev was only prepared to accept 80. As Tsessarsky recalled, 'It was a difficult task, people got angry if rejected and tried to lie to get into the platoon.' Those successful candidates would go to form the nucleus of the 'Winners', one of several partisan formations being created from OMSBON members. Each group was allotted or chose a code name, which would form part of their radio call sign. It had been decided to transport the 'Winners' behind enemy lines by air in several small groups. At this point Medvedev and his immediate staff were made aware of the long-term object of their mission.

The advance guard of the 'Winners' was landed at a partisan airstrip near Briansk but almost immediately was betrayed to the Germans and executed. Tsessarsky's section followed on 10 June 1942. Along with some 14 others he was flown in. The group reported their successful arrival to Moscow by radio and the next group, including Boris Chorny, arrived several days later. Shortly after they linked up and Medvedev's troops were engaged

This anti-tank rifle, PTRD Model 1941 had a calibre of 14.5mm and was a single-shot weapon effective against soft-skinned vehicles but also as a sniper's weapon. The ammunition case and rounds are visible to the right. Weighing in at 17kg it was robust and simple to maintain but unwieldy at 2m long. (Courtesy of the Central Museum of the Armed Forces Moscow via www.stavka.org.uk)

in their first encounter with the Germans. Anatoly Kapchinsky, a famous skater – one of the unit's many sportsmen, was killed in action on 28 June. Although they had undergone specialist training the members of OMSBON really learned about life when on campaign. As an OMSBON report later noted, 'It was necessary to [learn] everything you need on the farm: to build shelters and dugouts, light a fire, grind flour and bake bread, mend clothes and shoes. Make everything you need to harness a horse to a cart, weave sandals, cook dinner, milk a cow; dig a well and a lot more.'

In the absence of mine-detection gear partisan units resorted to more primitive methods as shown here – poking the ground with a sharp stick. The multi-purpose wire cutter could also be used to lever the mine out of the ground and to unscrew the fuse. (Courtesy of the Central Museum of the Armed Forces Moscow via www.stavka.org.uk)

Camp construction seems to have been a fairly standardized undertaking, varying only with the terrain. Defensive minefields were laid at some distance from the camp: within this perimeter patrols and sentries would be deployed. Trenches and machine-gun nests were dug. The best, long-term sites were always near running water to provide not only drink but laundry and bathing facilities. As a rule the centre of the camp was the staff dugout and the hospital facility. Around these were placed the residential bunkers. Workshops were established for weapons repair, carpentry, sewing and of course cooking. Stables and latrines were posted at a convenient distance from the living quarters for reasons of sanitation. If the camp was destined for long-term habitation then training grounds were prepared including shooting ranges

 D

PARTISAN TASKS

Day-to-day partisan activities included the following.

1. Destroying telephone/telegraph wires. The man simply smashes the insulators with an axe butt. He is wearing a padded jacket, *telogreika*, fur cap and felt, *valenki*, boots. Having cut the wires and smashed the insulators the partisans would often lie in wait for the repair crews and ambush them. Lengths of cable were often recycled by the partisans or strung between trees to catch unwary horsemen or motorcyclists.

2. Spreading news and propaganda by the simple expedient of nailing up a poster, often in the local dialect, could be hazardous. When paper was unavailable birch bark was a good substitute. Charcoal was used for the writing. This method of spreading information was widely used and the vocabulary was kept to a very basic level often repeating familiar pre-war Soviet slogans. If caught doing such work the messenger was executed, gender and age were irrelevant to the occupation forces in such matters.

3. Sitting and watching enemy movements was a vital, if dull, method of intelligence gathering. Sometimes relays of observers would work on a shift system keeping a tally record of the types of vehicle, numbers of men, animals and equipment passing along a particular route. Specialists in this type of work became adept at recognizing Axis unit markings such as divisional emblems and tactical symbols. Certainly from 1943 onwards the German staff tried to restrict the use of many such symbols as a security measure but with little apparent success.

4. Executing a collaborator, with his brassard denoting his function, was frequently employed to reinforce the Soviet regime's authority in occupied areas. Such activities were not uncommon. Few, if any, prisoners were kept alive after interrogation and executions were often performed in public with local civilian onlookers encouraged to bear witness to such acts of justice and revenge. If local collaborators were seen by their victims to receive punishment where they had carried out their traitorous activities what better way of demonstrating the speed and efficacy of Soviet retribution? Following an area's liberation such actions were widespread and usually involved group hangings in a city's central square.

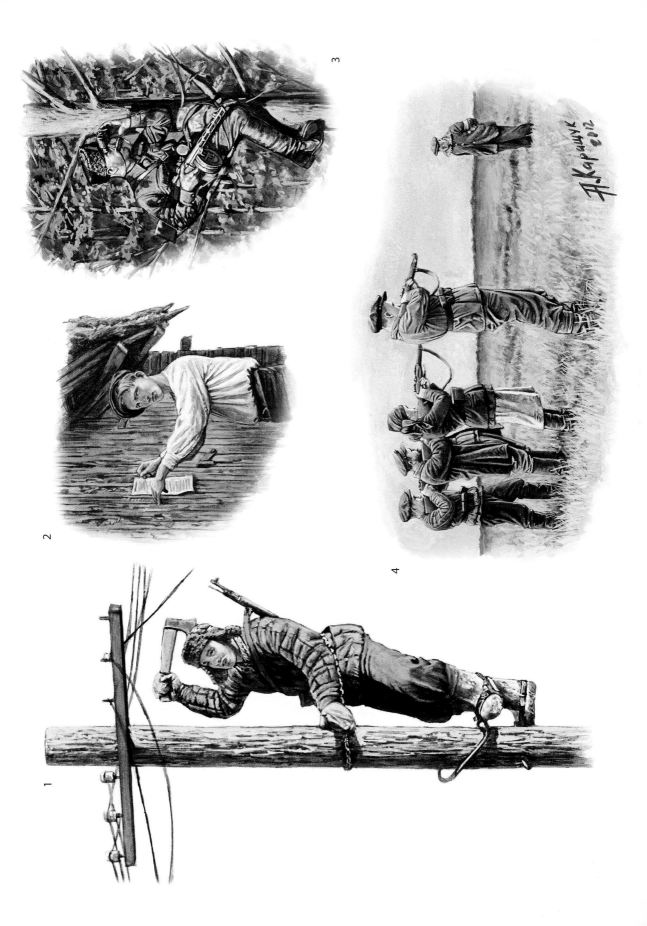

Kovpak's men took great pride in their artillery detachment. Two 76mm Model 1927 guns were flown in during October 1942. Specifically designed for close infantry support they were nicknamed 'Stalin'. The transport method is shown here and both pieces had their shields removed when on the march. Their use was strictly controlled due to ammunition re-supply issues. (From the fonds of the RGAKFD, Kranogorsk via www.stavka.org.uk)

and assault courses. Airstrips, capable of taking cargo planes, necessitated flat ground clear of undergrowth.

A major result of the early months that OMSBON units were on campaign was the analysis of reports fed back to Moscow. These provided a steep learning curve for the base staff. A committee for the study and reporting on these documents was set up and met for the first of many sittings in August 1942. The field reports pulled no punches and highlighted several shortcomings that included personnel and equipment amongst other things.

The poor quality of some unit leaders only became apparent at the point of insertion when the behaviour displayed was not as it should have been, including 'weakness of character', a euphemism for cowardice: poor leadership skills and a lack of tactical awareness were others. The committee was disappointed but pleased that these traits had come to light before the men were beyond Moscow's control. One officer, who failed at this point, redeemed himself when attached to a different unit, others were lost in action. Several commanders were 'trying apparently, to establish [their] authority and, without trial, without evidence of guilt men were sentenced to death'. There were three executions as a result of these wrongdoings in the 'Voroshilov' and 'Cousin' units. 'Spontaneously created field Court Martials' had taken place in other groups. No mention was made of the fates of the officers concerned.

For the campaign in western Ukraine Kovpak's unit was issued with 11 45mm M1937 anti-tank guns, effective against light armour and soft-skinned vehicles. Comparatively light and robust, these guns did not fire high explosives but did have canister ability. (Courtesy of the Central Museum of the Armed Forces Moscow via www.stavka.org.uk)

Criticism of equipment was widespread. The size and weight of radios and batteries had resulted in 'some cases each soldier had to carry from 40 to 50kgs of cargo', this often in addition to their own kit. 'This made the troops immobile, inactive.' The loss of radios forced a 'special squad' of 13 men to abort its mission prematurely. The Mosin-Nagant rifle was found to be too cumbersome and the lack of boots had led, during the previous winter, to 'frequent cases of frostbite'.

Physically and mentally some of the men were found not to be up to the demands imposed on them by partisan warfare, despite unit doctors' best efforts to weed them out during the initial screening process. Later reports dating from 1943–44 commented that the demands of the staff in Moscow 'were taken without regard for the real situation. In these cases [HQ] was not always aware of the physical condition of the soldiers and commanders, many of which had endured 18 months to two years on the move without a break in the enemy's rear and are in desperate need of psychological relaxation and rest.' The author of this report was clearly a man who cared deeply about the men and women under his command and was unhesitating in his not so veiled criticism of his superiors. It is hard to imagine an officer in the regular

Security forces were often issued captured weapons. This group has been equipped with a Czech-made ZB-30 light machine gun. The central figure is carrying what appears to be another Czech weapon, the ZK/383 sub-machine gun. The others carry the standard-issue rifles. (Nik Cornish@ www.stavka.org.uk)

Red Army who would have dared to put pen to paper with such blunt comments. Indeed it sums up the relationships that developed in small units that an officer was prepared to speak out on behalf of his troops so. The report went to note several instances of desertion due to stress. That men or women of the NKVD could do such a thing was almost unthinkable, as they had virtually condemned their families to imprisonment or worse. The regime may have allowed their partisan units a degree of independence, even licence, but desertion in the face of the enemy was unpardonable.

Although insertion was usually made by air, in January 1944 an opportunity arose when the lines were particularly fluid so it was decided to try another method. Eight Studebaker trucks drove to a point 60km behind the German front carrying some 50 men and five tons of equipment. The attempt was successful but the rest of the journey had to be made on skis with the equipment carried on sledges. Partisan life was nothing if not physical.

BELIEF AND BELONGING

The USSR in 1941 was a land-based empire with a population in excess of 160,000,000 from 100 widely differing ethnic backgrounds, speaking dozens of languages. The previous 27 years had been a time of turmoil; war, revolution,

Inside a workshop dugout partisans carry out routine cleaning and maintenance of the weapons, two PPS-42 sub-machine guns are visible. (Courtesy of the Central Museum of the Armed Forces Moscow via www.stavka.org.uk)

economic upheaval and famine had devastated what, in 1914, had been a prosperous and rapidly developing state. The dominant people were the Russians and each individual was classified on their personal identity documentation according to their ethnicity. Although there had been considerable migration to the cities and developing industrial areas in the years leading up to the outbreak of war, the majority of the population still dwelt in the countryside and worked on the land. With the absorption of the Baltic States, Bessarabia and western Ukraine from 1939 to 1940 a considerable population of anti-Soviet, anti-Russian people had come under Soviet control. Collectivization and Russification

had been undertaken to bring these nationalities to heel but progress had been slow despite the deportation and imprisonment of large numbers of the more obvious potential troublemakers. Nor were the western borderlands the only area of concern for the regime in Moscow. There had been sporadic outbreaks of unrest in the Asian provinces as well as the Caucasus during the pre-war years.

Stalin's government was well aware of the simmering undercurrent of discontent. However, it was only during the first weeks of Operation *Barbarossa* that it became clear that this problem was a serious threat to the integrity of the Soviet state. It was obvious that measures had to be taken to generate unity and a common purpose to motivate the disparate groups across the Soviet Union to fight for the regime's survival.

Stalin's broadcast on 3 July 1941 set the tone for a national struggle by including the ethnic groups that were under threat from fascist aggression.

E

ACTS OF SABOTAGE

Mine warfare was an obviously important partisan tactic as traffic interdiction underpinned many of their operations, particularly after the order of 5 September 1942. During the summer of 1943 various partisan formations participated in Operation *Rail War* designed to interrupt the German supply chain across the entire Eastern Front but specifically Heeresgruppe Mitte. Its follow-up Operation *Concert* aimed to disrupt the retreat of Heeresgruppe Mitte following the failure of the Kursk offensive.

The devices shown in figures 3 and 4 were designed with partisan operations in mind by Colonel I. G. Starinov. The majority of the mines did not have an official designation as they fell outside of normal munitions production and supply chain. Orders were placed with specific manufacturers by the CHQPM for specific units. In most cases the explosive charges were too small to do more than weaken a section of railway. Therefore they were placed at the point where two rails abutted.

1. The mine shown here is for use with a length of Bickford fuse (slow burning) or an electric blasting cap. Generally used when its discovery by security patrols, seeing the smoke, was unlikely it was ideal for destroying unguarded objectives. The model shown here has an electric blasting cap consisting of a blasting cap and an electric detonator. However, the electrical method was unpopular due to the extra equipment involved with the detonator alone weighing 7kg.

2. Using fig 1 to weaken a wooden bridge with a Bickford fuse.

3. A simple to make mine that was finally assembled in situ. The effect was similar to that of figure 5. Detonation occurred when the train wheel runs over the blasting cap and fuse cord.

4. This mine was widely used from 1942 onwards. A charge of up to 1kg was attached to or buried beneath a section of rail line. Two electrical wires running from a small battery were tied to the top of the track. When a steel wheel ran over it the circuit was completed and the resulting explosion was sufficient to derail the train. A major drawback was that it would not work in temperatures lower than -5 C. Furthermore batteries were in very short supply.

5. Developed in 1942 this mine, sometimes nicknamed the 'sassy mine' was often manufactured by partisan units from scrap to which then added an MD-2 fuse and explosives. A 600g charge could blow a hole 10 x 7.5cm in a piece of track. Thus weakened, the weight of the locomotive or heavily laden wagons would snap the track and derail the train. Detonation was caused by the weight, only 1kg, depressing the P-shaped linchpin into the fuse

6. Anti-vehicle mine PDM 1. Inside the wooden case are two blocks of TNT weighing 800g. Detonation happened when the rod on the top was depressed once or twice with a time lapse of up to five minutes depending on the setting. This allowed for the often empty truck pushed ahead of the locomotive to pass over thus avoiding a premature explosion. If the operator decided that no first pressure by the target was required he would make the first depression himself. The pressure required for activation was 4kg.

7. Two demolition men bury pressure-detonated mines under a railway track while one man keeps watch. This method was popular as long as there was time to camouflage and enclose the mine, often with clay, so that the blast's power was channelled.

The Sixth Partisan Brigade, Leningrad area, receives its flag on 23 February 1944 – the annual holiday commemorating the foundation of the Red Army in 1918. (Courtesy of the Central Museum of the Armed Forces Moscow via www.stavka.org.uk)

Constructing a winter dugout, a *Zemlyanka*, in less than ideal conditions. The partisans' manual specified these should be capable of housing six people and have an emergency exit in case of attack. (Courtesy of the Central Museum of the Armed Forces Moscow via www.stavka.org.uk)

The underlying message was simple – everyone is in this together and it is imperative that we present a unified front.

The Red Army was overwhelmingly composed of Slavs for the simple reason that the authorities did not fully trust other ethnic groups. Using the army as an ethnic melting pot had always been a feature of Soviet policy, the words of command were Russian, the oath was sworn to the 'people, the Soviet Motherland and the Workers-Peasants Government', in other words the USSR and the Communist Party respectively. Before 1914 the concept of the Motherland, the *Rodina*, was not deeply rooted in Russian consciousness but the Party had made considerable steps, following its assumption of power in 1918, to develop the idea of parallel loyalty to Party and homeland. Stalin was to develop this further by calling on and encouraging the sense of Russian unity by making little or no direct reference to fighting for the regime but fighting for the Motherland instead. The symbolic figure of Mother Russia featured widely in poster campaigns particularly from 1941 to 1943. Identifying oneself as first a Soviet citizen then a Georgian, Galician or Ukrainian was of paramount importance during the early years of the war when victory was not inevitable.

When Chorny mentioned dying for one's country he did not mention the Party or belief in a better system of government and he meant precisely what he said. His motivation for joining up was simple patriotism. That he believed the Soviet system to be better than that of the invaders was implicit but not assumed. German methodology – be it industrial, agricultural or scientific – had been regarded as superior to the Russian equivalents for well over a century. The admiration previously extended to French culture and military expertise had gradually been replaced by that of Germany. The military superiority of Germany had been writ large during World War I and the speed with which the Poles, French and British had been defeated during 1940 had merely reinforced the point. In some quarters Germany was viewed as invincible and it was this psychological edge that needed to be blunted.

When the men and women of OMSBON witnessed at first hand the failure of the German Army before the gates of Moscow it demonstrated to them that they were capable of scoring victories. As news of the German defeat spread across the Little Land it stiffened the resolve of the isolated partisan bands struggling to survive the winter; it proved that there was a purpose to their suffering. For men like Kovpak and Rudnev, both relatively politically sophisticated, there was a strong belief in Communism that vied with simple patriotism and the basic human instinct to defend their home and family from outside aggressors. For the bulk of the civilian partisans it was the combination of instinctive self-defence and patriotism that motivated them to join the struggle behind the lines.

The famous Panzer general Heinz Guderian recorded a meeting with a retired Tsarist general, an anti-Communist, in Orel during 1941, who commented, 'If you had come 20 years ago we would have welcomed you … now it is too late… Now we are fighting for Russia and in that case we're all united.'

Concerts, lectures, film shows and the celebration of national holidays were always high points for both partisans and their civilian guests. (Courtesy of the Central Museum of the Armed Forces Moscow via www.stavka.org.uk)

However, no amount of flag waving, speech making and coercion or training exercises, whether imposed from on high or developed through the unavoidable intimacy of barrack or camp life, can weld any unit together like the jointly experienced combination of emotions that constitutes surviving a battle. Knowing who to trust to keep you covered, clear a weapon stoppage coolly and carefully under fire and who doesn't crack under the strain of night after night behind enemy lines; these are all elements that engender a sense of group identity. Although men may have played in the same team, worked at the same machine or lived in the same street and been friends from childhood, combat is an entirely different matter.

In addition to the shared experience of battle the partisans, almost without exception, witnessed on virtually a daily basis the horrific reality, the inhumanity of the regime operating in the occupied areas. Burnt-out villages, convoys of impressed workers heading west, the mutilated corpses of civilians old and young – the simple facts of ethnic cleansing – were ever present. The desire for revenge, pure and simple, welded many a partisan group from top to bottom.

Unless of sufficient importance to be airlifted to Moscow for further interrogation POWs were generally executed. The despondency on these men's faces tells its own story. (Courtesy of the Central Museum of the Armed Forces Moscow via www.stavka.org.uk)

Symbolism, such as the use of flags, was exploited to foster a sense of pride and belonging. Kovpak's unit flew a locally made flag from late 1941; others were issued from the CHQPM. Identifying with the leader was common; *Medvedevtsi* and *Kovpakovtsi* were the affectionate terms for Medvedev's people and Kovpak's people. The term expresses a deeper connection, akin to follower, and was more commonly used by the locals than 'Winners'.

The upsurge in partisan recruitment following the German surrender at Stalingrad and then the defeat at Kursk came as no surprise to the old hands who treated the newcomers with the

wariness of any veteran uncertain of the ability of the new recruit on whom he may have to depend. The same situation was repeated on a much wider scale as the success of Operation *Bagration* became obvious.

EXPERIENCE OF BATTLE

The men and women of both the 'Winners' and Kovpak's force had been lucky inasmuch as they were not participants in a brutal, large-scale engagement. Each was gradually introduced to battle. For the 'Winners' it was their involvement as what could be described as onlookers during the defence of Moscow, whereas Kovpak's unit had fought a series of small-scale skirmishes.

However, all this was to change when, separately, they were assigned specific missions that would take them far from their homes into an environment where death and destruction were almost everyday experiences. The bulk of the rank and file had no concept of the harsh truths of warfare, nor did they have more than a vague idea of what their missions were. They simply understood that they were taking their brand of warfare deep into the 'Temporarily Occupied Territories' and that they were striking back at the enemy, not merely holding on. Although none would experience anything that resembled the great set-piece battles such as Borodino, Gettysburg or Sedan, their battles would drag on for days or be over so quickly that they were difficult to recall.

UNDERCOVER OPERATIONS

One of the 'Winners' major tasks was to eliminate the Reichskommissar for the Ukraine, Erich Koch. To this end an NKVD operative, N. I. Kuznetsov, was parachuted in to join them on 26 August 1942. Just over two months later Kuznetsov made his first visit to Rivne, Koch's Ukrainian capital in the guise of Leutnant Paul Siebert. To perfect his already remarkable command of German, Kuznetsov had spent several weeks posing as a German POW in NKVD Camp 27 located in suburban Moscow at Krasnogorsk.

Two attempts on Koch were aborted due to the high level of his personal security. However, he was not the only target, nor was execution Kuznetsov's only purpose. During each visit he made to Rivne disguised as Siebert, Kuznetsov was also gathering intelligence. During the spring of 1943 Kuznetsov confirmed that the Germans were planning to attack at Kursk and that Hitler's command post, codenamed 'Werewolf', for the Eastern Front was located at Vinnitsa.

Under orders from Moscow Kuznetsov was instructed to execute Koch's deputy Paul Dargel. Dargel lived in Schloss Strasse in Rivne, a heavily guarded, residential area reserved for German officials. Poles and Ukrainians were not allowed in this area for security reasons. A local partisan informer, who worked for the administration, had informed Kuznetsov of Dargel's daily routine and it was decided to carry out the mission on 20 September 1943. As he left his office for home at 1430hrs Kuznetsov would kill him. Kuznetsov had been told that Dargel was always accompanied by his adjutant who carried a red leather attaché case. Furthermore when he left the Reichskommissariat he was always preceded by a military policeman who would check the way was clear. Arriving just before the appointed time in a light brown Opel Captain car, Kuznetsov did not have long to wait. Jumping from the car Kuznetsov saw the two men plus attaché case and, as they turned around hearing footsteps, fired three shots into each man. His driver, NKVD operative Nikolai Strutinski, gunned the accelerator and they sped off.

Two days later the local papers reported the incident. It was then that Kuznetsov, at the 'Winners' base, discovered that it was not Dargel and his assistant he had executed but a senior economist, Hans Gehl. One month later Kuznetsov's second attempt on Dargel, this time with anti-tank grenades, succeeded in hospitalizing him with severe leg injuries that led to both being amputated.

One of the most important facets of the 'Winners' mission was to support an NKVD assassin's task – the execution of Erich Koch, *Reichskommissar* for Ukraine. The operative who was to carry out this job was N. I. Kuznetsov, aka Lieutenant P. W. Seibert. Koch lived in the capital of occupied Ukraine, Rivne (Rovno) in western Ukraine, therefore it was to this area that the 'Winners' were sent. As with all other OMSBON operations there was a wider agenda. They were expected to gather intelligence, commit acts of sabotage, recruit and organize satellite partisan units and remind the population of the omnipresence of the Soviet regime and its anticipated return.

During the early summer of 1942 the component units of the 'Winners' were parachuted into eastern Ukraine to begin their trek to the west. They walked using the 'guerrilla step' that is in single file treading on the footsteps of the person in front; a rear-guard followed removing traces of their progress. The Sarny Forest, through which their march led them, was damp and the undergrowth thick while the air swarmed with clouds of mosquitoes. 'We walked at night and during the day rested on the ground. We got wet in the swamps and in the pouring rain, two kilometres on the map turned into five on the ground.' Sometimes the scouts would send a message halting the column due to something suspicious and then it was hard to move on. Horses and wagons had been requisitioned but it proved necessary to lead the horses and manhandle the wagons as the going was so bad. Tsessarsky recalled continually 'dressing bloody blisters' and reminding men about keeping their feet healthy.

Another dozen men, including Kuznetsov, joined them, bringing their strength by the end of July up to almost 100 men and women.

When they eventually arrived in the Rivne area they established their base deep in the nearby forests. It was from here that small groups would venture out to attack police posts, convoys and railway lines. Often led by local guides the number of partisans involved varied depending on the mission, that was usually undertaken based on intelligence reports from their own scouts or trustworthy locals.

The destruction of railway lines and the consequent disruption to supply flow was the main activity of many partisan units. This was carried out by the simple expedient of burning wooden bridges, mining the track or loosening it sufficiently to cause a derailment. The latter operation involved three or four men tying a strong rope to the loose track and pulling it out of alignment just as the locomotive was about to run over it. Wire from telegraph/telephone lines that ran trackside was also used to this end.

Collecting intelligence was often a matter of sitting, watching and counting alongside a railway or road. The photo shows one of Kovpak's scouts taking advantage of some shade. (Courtesy of the Central Museum of the Armed Forces Moscow via www.stavka.org.uk)

Roadside ambushes generally followed a set pattern of which this is a typical example. A convoy of ten trucks was gathering supplies from a series of villages that lay within a few kilometres of one another. Neither the route followed nor the timings had altered since the round was established almost a year before. The drivers were all former Red Army men now *Hiwis*. The escort of some 20 indigenous Ukrainian *Schutzmannschaft* (literally translated as defence troops: locally raised collaborationist auxiliary police/security forces often abbreviated to Schuma) was commanded by a German police NCO, with maybe an officer and interpreter. Very occasionally a captured Soviet armoured car brought up the rear.

Three 'Winners' sections, roughly 50 men, were tasked with the ambush; they were under instructions to capture a German for interrogation. It was generally assumed that no POWs were taken other than for that reason as partisan formations had no POW facilities nor could they risk an escapee who might jeopardize their security. They decided to attack the convoy at

The execution of two collaborators. The partisans acted as the agents of the Soviet regime in such matters. To the right of the condemned a staff officer reads out the sentence as the unit looks on. Only one grave has been dug and the firing party appears to consist of one. (From the fonds of the RGAKFD, Kranogorsk via www.stavka.org.uk)

a point where the dirt road dipped towards a narrow ford and the trucks tended to bunch up before crossing singly. Having reached the ambush spot positions were allocated. As the first and last vehicles were to be disabled by machine-gun fire, one DP machine-gun team supported by three riflemen took post on the far bank of the stream. A similar team was positioned 150m up the track. The command post was some 50m from the road with a good view of the area. A group of five or six men took up position beyond the roadside machine-gun nest; they were armed with anti-tank grenades and Molotov cocktails to deal with the armoured car if necessary. If it did not appear then they were to sweep along the convoy herding the survivors towards the ford. The remaining men hid in the undergrowth at intervals along the roadside between the machine-gun posts. Firing was to begin simultaneously, the sign being a flare fired from the command post. Once in position the men waited. One recalled, 'My comrade and I took turns to doze. We were so still, like stones. We were not nervous just full of anticipation.' A bird defecated on the disc magazine of the machine gun and one of the team had to struggle with his trousers – for obvious reasons.

> We only waited 90 minutes but it seemed like longer without a smoke. Then the fascists came and it all happened so fast. I did not see the flare but fired at my target, the third lorry driver. He died instantly. The noise was overwhelming as just before it had been the engines idling in a line, then the sound of all the weapons going off. I reloaded, a new clip, my comrade was cursing, his PPD had jammed, an unheard of event. Then we heard our battle cry 'Urrah' as the sweepers went into action. There was no armoured car. Our men had stopped firing so we flankers went into the fight. I used a short (cut down) bayonet in such situations. The police fought but most died in the first volleys. Then it was all over. No one could find the Germans, or any paperwork. We always gathered trophy weapons and checked the bodies for information. Two sweepers had injuries but they were slight, nevertheless we applied field dressings to prevent infection.

Tsessarsky was insistent regarding the speedy treatment of any wound, however slight, to maintain everyone's combat effectiveness. 'The sappers rigged some of the vehicles with booby traps, grenades.'

With the mission partially accomplished they rallied at the command post and set off for the last village the convoy had visited. On arrival there

PARTISANS IN COMBAT

Partisans in action. From small-scale attacks on convoys to larger operations involving hundreds of combatants, taking the fight to the occupation forces was the prime objective of the partisan forces.

1. This attack on a German convoy, during the first winter campaign, shows an ill-considered operation. Experience would teach that it would be prudent to ambush this convoy before they could emerge from the trees. Immobilizing the first and last vehicles in line would have prevented easy movement and provided a row of 'sitting ducks'. As it stands this group of partisans will be hard pressed to inflict many losses let alone make good their escape.

2. Axis security forces recruited large numbers of collaborators to police the vast rural areas behind the lines. During 1942–43 these police outposts found themselves surrounded by an increasingly hostile population. If their communications were cut such groups would be ideal targets for the partisans. Here a well-armed partisan detachment is in the process of overrunning a police unit in a forest village.

Protecting civilians against retaliation was sometimes a necessity and certainly a useful propaganda exercise. Here a partisan unit evacuates a village. (Courtesy of the Central Museum of the Armed Forces Moscow via www.stavka.org.uk)

was no sign of the armoured car or the Germans. When the villagers were questioned they said the convoy had been sent ahead while the Germans had stayed elsewhere sampling the local moonshine.

Larger engagements were almost always provoked by major Axis anti-partisan operations. These were very different in character as the Germans' security forces were developing their tactics as a result of their experiences. Generally they attempted to encircle a partisan base and then draw the circle tighter and tighter until their troops converged at a central point. The 'Winners' were the subject of such an attack in early November 1943.

Medvedev's force had by this time facilitated the development of several smaller units in the area. All were sending representatives to the 'Winners" new winter quarters to celebrate the anniversary of the Bolshevik revolution of November 1917. However, as the celebrations got underway little did they know but their location had been disclosed to the Germans by a renegade partisan. Medvedev was informed by a runner from one of his outposts that security units were assembling nearby and that an early morning attack was likely. Mounting the stage as a Charlie Chaplin impersonator finished his turn Medvedev explained the situation to the audience declaring, 'First we defeat the enemy, then leave – the holiday will continue!' Such a display of confidence by their leader was sufficient for most of the men to sleep with a degree of calm. Sentries were doubled, those not on duty slept fully clothed with their weapons close at hand. Medvedev outlined his plan to the staffs present. The 750 men at his disposal were divided into four companies. The Second Company was sent on a wide outflanking march, the object of which was to get into the rear of the enemy, specifically their artillery lines and command centre. The flanks of the camp were to be held by the Fourth Company; the north face of the camp, from which direction the main attack was anticipated, was the responsibility of the First Company. The rear, south face, would be held by the Third Company. A reserve was formed by the 'Winners' scout platoon.

The attack began when the autumn mist dispersed at around 1000hrs. As anticipated the north was the main point of attack. The security troops came on, pushing through heavy undergrowth, firing randomly in an effort to provoke a response. When the First Company opened fire with machine guns the Germans went to ground, a situation replicated on the flanks. The probing attack gave the German gunners and mortar teams a good idea of the range and they opened fire using the short-barrelled 75mm light infantry gun and 81mm mortars.

As the smoke swirled between the trees and shrapnel mixed with vicious shards of pine and birch trees, the partisans kept their heads down 'eating the earth'. A survivor of the battle remembered, 'The cries of the wounded mingled with the detonations of the mortar bombs amongst our party site.' When the Germans switched targets or ceased fire an occasional probing attack went in to be met with withering volleys always held until the last possible moment for maximum effect. Ammunition and water were sent to

A successful night operation by the 'Winners' results in severe damage to a bridge. (Courtesy of the Central Museum of the Armed Forces Moscow via www.stavka.org.uk)

the firing lines as often as possible, the men crawling forward, hugging cover with their loads of bandoliers and water bottles. However, as the wounded were dragged back to receive attention and replacements were sent in the situation began to look increasingly bad. As the afternoon drew on it was necessary to commit the reserves in a number of counterattacks. No quarter was given or asked as men fought vicious micro-battles for a machine-gun pit or a couple of metres of slit trench, biting, hacking and slashing at one another in the smoke and increasing gloom. 'Sometimes you only identified your enemy when they were swinging at you or the flash of gunshots briefly lit up your line of sight.' As the light faded, Medvedev called for the less serious casualties to return to the fight. Tsessarsky noted that, 'I and all the medical staff were wounded.' By 1800hrs German pressure was such that the order was given to hitch up the wagons and load them with wounded to prepare to break out under cover of darkness. No help from other units was likely and it appeared that the Second Company had failed in its mission to the enemy rear. 'I was clearly aware that if we did not hold out until dark

Kovpak, fourth from left in hat, enjoys a meal with his staff in the house of a local priest who is seated at the head of the table. (From the fonds of the RGAKFD, Kranogorsk via www.stavka.org.uk)

The culmination of the partisan war was the parade in celebration of the liberation of Minsk, capital of Belarus on 17 July 1944. Here the colour parties of some of the units represented pass the saluting base. The salute was taken by General P. K. Ponomarenko, who had been head of the Central HQ of the Partisan Movement from 1942 to 1944. Their last order was to prepare for disbandment. (Courtesy of the Central Museum of the Armed Forces Moscow via www.stavka.org.uk)

then we could not escape the Germans' Medvedev wrote later. 'Then we distinctly heard the Russian "Hurrah". It was the Second Company going into the attack.' It had taken the Second Company the best part of ten hours to work its way around the German flank and into their rear. However, when they arrived they could clearly see the gun and mortar positions some 200m

EXTEMPORISED WEAPONS

Several partisan units were lucky to have creative minds available that were capable of turning out weapons from unlikely sources such as those shown here. Well-established units developed small light industrial workshops equipped with machine tools capable of repairing and maintaining small arms. Fortunate were those units that recruited machinists or engineers.

1 Very similar in appearance to the PPSh this sub-machine gun was designed by E. Martynjuka and used by the unit 'In the name of Molotov' that operated in the Pinsk region.

2–6 A variety of one-off models created by various partisan groups and incorporating items from a variety of sources.

7 Designed by N. Sergeev and used by the 'Banner' unit this sub-machine gun has the standard 7.62mm calibre of Soviet weapons.

8 Used by partisan brigade 'Thunderstorm' in the Vitebsk area this weapon was designed by V. N. Dolganov, an artilleryman. Before the invasion Dolganov had been an engineer and used his skills to create this weapon which combined features from several other sub machine guns. Effective to a range of 500m with a calibre of 7.62mm it was fed by a 71-round drum magazine.

9 As used by a unit in the Minsk region this is a Shavgulidze rifle grenade launcher. The grenade can be seen above.

10 Two types of an ancient weapon used to disable horses – the caltrop. They could be deployed against vehicles, men or horses.

11 Removed from the turret of a T-50 tank this 20K 45mm M1938 gun has been mounted on a steel-wheeled chassis taken from a piece of agricultural machinery. The gun is capable of firing armour-piercing and fragmentation rounds.

12 A 37mm mortar tube has been based on an entrenching tool and given a bipod made from steel rods.

13 A simple bent steel tripod mounting for a Maxim M1910 machine gun.

14 This Maxim M1910 machine gun on its normal Sokolov wheeled mount has had its barrel modified with a homemade air cooling system to replace the water jacket.

from the command post. The commander split his force into two; one overran the command post and the other the gun lines where they turned the mortars on the attackers. With the tables so rapidly turned and effectively leaderless the security troops broke off their attack and fell back in disorder to whatever defensible positions they could find.

With the encirclement broken the partisans regrouped, counted their trophies and under cover of darkness pulled out from their now compromised base. A small party was left behind to cover the move and then make off in a different direction to distract any would be pursuers. The main body trekked off into the night in search of safe winter quarters. As Medvedev put it, 'It was a pity to leave such a nice place to freeze in the cold and get wet in the rain but there was no alternative.' However, they had achieved the objective – to live to fight another day. News of such successful actions did much to raise the profile and prestige of the partisans and prove yet again that the Germans were not invincible. When the daily radio contact with Moscow was made later that day the 'Winners' received the news that Kiev had been liberated – yet another victory to let the local population know of.

When P. P. Vershigora was sent by Moscow to join Kovpak's intelligence unit as an officer but also a photographer it was just before they set out on the trans-Dnieper expedition in 1942. The purpose of this operation was to establish a partisan presence in this hitherto relatively quiet area. Vershigora's role did not preclude him joining combat missions; indeed he was expected to join in, despite having seen combat before he had yet to prove his worth to his new comrades. He was attached to the Thirteenth Company, who he described as 'candidate guerrillas' as they were also unproven. They were ordered to carry out a simple ambush and destroy a bridge.

It is believed that this image shows the news printers of the 'Voroshilov' unit. The lady in the overall is possibly Tsila Dolinko, the man to the extreme right her husband Ayreh. Both had escaped from the Pinsk ghetto. The man in the *pilotka* may be Ignazi Baspromni, who was flown in from Moscow to edit the Polish and Ukrainian language editions. Behind is the entrance to their dugout. (Courtesy of the Central Museum of the Armed Forces Moscow via www.stavka.org.uk)

Having mined the bridge and established a command post the men took up positions on either side of the road in the undergrowth. The ground had been cleared of vegetation for some 50m on either side in order to discourage ambushes such as this. Vershigora recalled, 'Guys, tired of incessant marching slept. And I dozed off.' Awoken by a noise he 'parted the bushes and saw two large trucks and a passenger car … approaching the bridge'. He alerted the others just as the car hit a mine and the convoy halted. Simultaneously the partisans opened fire. Those Germans that could jumped out of their vehicles to take cover. Followed by several others, Vershigora crossed the open ground towards the road, dodging from cover to cover. Although briefly pinned down by machine-gun fire, they advanced again when it was silenced. Warily the partisans approached the trucks, which seemed empty. Then, as the smoke cleared, Vershigora saw 'in a shallow ditch, crawled something green. It was the Germans or rather the bottoms of the Germans! Boys hit them! And we began to shoot.' There was no return fire. 'I was seized by a fit of mischief and pulled out the camera, pointed it at one of the Nazis who was trying to escape. Suddenly a strong push from behind knocked me down. I found out after the battle when I wanted to take the picture another under a truck went to shoot at me.' Vershigora's life had been saved by one of the company's scouts. 'We became firm friends from that day onwards; it was based on mutual respect and gratitude.'

Destroying railway lines was a time-consuming job. The area would be secured and the rails dismantled. A fire would be started and then the lines heated to the point where they could be bent and twisted. (Courtesy of the Central Museum of the Armed Forces Moscow via www.stavka.org.uk)

Vershigora remained with Kovpak and it was he that returned from Moscow on 12 June 1943 with orders to launch what has become known as the Carpathian Raid. During this operation they marched, 3,000 strong, across western Ukraine with the objective of pushing into the Carpathian Mountains and spreading the partisan war deeper into occupied Europe.

Having spent some time in the vicinity of Rivne, where they encountered the 'Winners', they proceeded south-west. Their march had been monitored by the intelligence and security forces in the area but efforts to engage them had come to nothing as they were moving swiftly and the forces in the region were negligible. Whether this lack of opposition made the leadership complacent will never be known but nemesis was waiting for them at the town of Deliatyn in the Carpathian foothills. It was here that they fought what one veteran described as an encounter battle that, during the first week of August 1943, effectively destroyed Kovpak's force's cohesion. To cross into the town, where they intended to attack the local garrison, it was essential to cross a long, narrow bridge. As dawn approached the bridge guards were easily neutralized. However, the advance guard then seems to have fallen into a torpor, which may have been induced by fatigue. Several men immediately fell into a deep sleep and were left behind as the remainder moved off along the motor road towards the town, but soon men began

A captured detonator that was part of the equipment used by the NKVD to demolish large areas of central Kiev following its capture in September 1941. This was attached to four tons of explosive. This event was the largest urban act of sabotage carried out by the NKVD and resulted in the deaths of hundreds of German troops and the reduction of the city centre to rubble. (Nik Cornish@ www.stavka.org.uk)

to straggle. Behind them the main body, including the baggage train of 300 or so wagons, was beginning to cross the bridge and a traffic jam building up. Meanwhile the advance guard came upon a seemingly abandoned line of German trucks just parked in the road. Somehow one of the partisans detonated a drum of fuel in one of the trucks at which point German troops, hidden nearby, opened fire. With the sun rising, seeing the smoke and hearing gunfire Kovpak ordered the main body to turn left off the road into a rye field in an attempt to organize support for the firing line and establish what was going on. Then the Luftwaffe struck, catching men and wagons in the open. Order broke down as every man headed for the nearest cover,

Men of Kovpak's unit dressing in captured items of clothing. There was an unfortunate 'friendly fire' incident when a group of Kovpak's men were ambushed by some of the 'Winners' near Rivne as they were clad in German-issue police uniforms. (From the fonds of the RGAKFD, Kranogorsk via www.stavka.org.uk)

particularly a forest across the fields. Men and wagons were shot and bombed, driverless wagons and panic-stricken teams carved their own route of devastation through the fleeing crowds as casualties bounced from the makeshift ambulances and horses were cut down by the dozen. With no hope of support, the advance guard attempted to cover the main force. Meanwhile the rear-guard blew the bridge at 1000hrs having ensured the passage of nearly all the vehicles and artillery. As they fell back they followed the route taken by the main body 'so easily as it was clearly marked by dead horses, spilled wagons, abandoned equipment and dead men'. As was expected they searched for any wounded. However, it proved an almost impossible task and doubtless several mercy killings were carried out. Vershigora found himself in command of 400 men that included 50 or so wounded. When they re-joined the main force in the forest it was a much dispirited unit which was to change its organization in response to the losses suffered. Six units were created from the one large formation and each was ordered to make its way to a specified point from where they would review the situation. The artillery was abandoned, as was much of the baggage, documents were burned and even the staff typewriter smashed. But, more tellingly, those too wounded to travel were left behind, reliant on the hospitality of the locals and whatever defensive measures they could take. The battle of Deliatyn demonstrated that partisans are at their most effective when operating in small groups, unencumbered by heavy weapons and a lengthy baggage train. Stealth and concealment are greater partisan attributes than the ability to plan an artillery barrage.

Vershigora took charge of one unit and was later granted command of what remained of Kovpak's once mighty force, which was now named 1st S. A. Kovpak Ukrainian Partisan Division in his honour. Kovpak, severely wounded himself, was flown back to Moscow during the autumn. Few of his men were that lucky.

One of Kovpak's (to the rear with bald head) young troops receives a medal from D. S. Korotchenko, a very senior Party functionary who visited the unit during the Carpathian Raid in the early summer of 1943. The medal recipient's name is unknown. (Courtesy of the Central Museum of the Armed Forces Moscow via www.stavka.org.uk)

A group of Belarusian partisans pose for the camera with their newly awarded medals. Boys, and girls as well, such as those shown here, were often orphans adopted by the unit. The boys carry carbines instead of full-sized rifles. (Courtesy of the Central Museum of the Armed Forces Moscow via www.stavka.org.uk)

AFTER THE BATTLE

Every partisan who survived the fight unscathed was naturally elated to be in one piece but saddened by the loss of comrades. Whenever possible the dead were buried with a short ceremony. However, when Rudnev was declared killed in action a eulogy was solemnly read by one of his friends. When it was finished Kovpak dismissed the representatives of the units present on parade, 'the instruction was carried out quietly, as if asked not ordered'.

The situation for the wounded depended on the availability of medicine, trained staff and the severity of the wound. Tsessarsky had to perform emergency surgery on a man whose wound had developed gangrene. Having lost his instruments in a marsh Tsessarsky extemporized. 'A two handed saw was altered and sterilized and the leg removed. Vodka was used as an anaesthetic.' Embarrassed that he had used mother curses in a unit where such language was not tolerated, the patient reported for punishment when able. The case was dismissed. Whenever possible those who were unlikely to recover sufficiently to return to active duty were airlifted back to Moscow or later in the war to Kiev.

Much post-action time was spent carrying out the domestic duties of camp life such as weapons maintenance, food preparation and guard duty. However, the hearts and minds campaign was never overlooked; OMSBON units were expected to interact with the locals as much as possible. They were particularly zealous in continuing the upkeep of Soviet traditions, culture, festivals and holidays, for example Mayday, International Women's Day, Red Army Day and, most significant of all, the anniversary of the Bolshevik Revolution each November. Christmas and New Year 1943–44 involved a concert for children of the nearby villages. 'Fighter Mansur was Santa Claus. The children quickly stopped being shy and were fascinated by a small Christmas tree, decorated with home-made toys, on top a five pointed star.' Documentary films, specially flown in, were shown repeatedly: a particular favourite was one entitled *The Defence of Moscow*. Newspapers were published and leaflets distributed in the appropriate local language, which were passed from village to village until they wore out. Countering German propaganda was deemed a high priority.

When not on duty partisans would paint, draw, read and write poetry, while some organized classes for their less literate comrades. But everyone wrote letters as, certainly for the OMSBON partisans, there were supply flights that carried in post. These were mainly sentimental, personal letters that were censored before departure lest the aircraft be shot down. Nevertheless mail call was a great boost to morale, helping to lift the spirits of even the most mentally exhausted.

To further improve morale special partisan medals were produced. Commanders were expected to put forward the names of those worthy to receive awards. Medvedev was made a Hero of the Soviet Union, the USSR's highest award, in November 1944. In February 1944 he was injured, and returned to Moscow. Just over a year later he was involved in fighting the Lithuanian nationalist partisan force known as the 'Forest Brothers'. Kovpak was twice made a Hero of the Soviet Union, once in 1942 and again in 1944.

MUSEUMS AND COLLECTIONS

Until the dissolution of the USSR during the early 1990s there were several museums that commemorated the partisan movement of the Great Patriotic War. Since that time local sentiment has led to their closure and the dispersal of the artefacts. In Ukraine, for example, items and exhibits commemorating the activities of Kuznetsov and Medvedev, lauded during the Soviet era, have been removed as a result of a backlash which appears to be based on the number of civilians who were executed in retaliation for partisan activities.

In Russia there is a major display at the Central Museum of the Armed Forces in Moscow. There is also a selection of partisan memorabilia at the Museum of the Great Patriotic War also in Moscow.

In Minsk the Belarusian State Museum for the Great Patriotic War has a large permanent exhibition devoted to partisan warfare in the region.

In Ukraine the Museum of Partisan Glory in the Spadshchansky Forest site near Putivl is of interest. However, the largest exhibition is in Kiev at the National Museum of the Great Patriotic War. Items on display include Kovpak's personal effects.

BIBLIOGRAPHY

Following the end of World War II there was a considerable outpouring of partisan memoirs, which continued for the next decade. Some were translated into English but these are virtually unobtainable at present. The memoirs of senior Soviet officers such as Rokossovsky and Zhukov, writing before the fall of Communism, toed the Party line and made token, glowing references to the partisans. However, since that time very little work has been done.

Blood, Philip W., *Hitler's Bandit Hunters*, Potomac Books: Washington DC, 2006

Cooper, Matthew, *Phantom War*, Macdonald and Jane's: London, 1979

Dallin, A., *German Rule in Russia*, Macmillan: London, 1957

Grau, Lester, and Gress, Michael, (editors) *The Partisan's Companion*, Casemate: Philadelphia and Newbury, 2011

Grenkevich, Leonid, *The Soviet Partisan Movement 1941–44*, Edited by David Glantz, Frank Cass, Oxford, 1999

Sudoplatov, Pavel, *Special Tasks*, Little, Brown & Co: London, 1994

During the Cold War the US armed forces used German officers' experiences to create at least two books on Soviet guerrilla tactics, presumably because they expected to encounter them. Interestingly one of the German contributors concluded that the only effective way to deal with partisans was the deployment of tactical nuclear weapons.

Combat in Russian Swamps and Marshes, Department of the Army pamphlet, US Army, 1951

The Soviet Partisan Movement, Department of the Army pamphlet, US Army, 1956

Moved from the countryside, this reconstructed partisan dugout is now part of the display at the Central Museum of the Armed Forces in Moscow. (Nik Cornish@ www.stavka.org.uk)

Some Jewish partisan units are covered by the following:

Duffy, Peter, *The Bielski Brothers*, Perennial paperback: London, 2004
Kagan, J., and Cohen, Dov, *Surviving the Holocaust with the Russian Jewish Partisans*, Vallentine Mitchell: London, 1998

The Internet has hundreds of sites of varying quality and usefulness. Unfortunately many of them fall into the trap of regurgitating the inflated claims made by some partisans, subsequently reinforced by Soviet historians, regarding the losses inflicted on the Axis supply network and manpower. However, the Jewish and Ukrainian nationalist aspects of the partisan war are covered in detail.

GLOSSARY

Words

Partisanshchina	sums up the qualities of a good partisan but suggests a certain deviation from the norms of Soviet society that is not altogether appropriate or desirable.
Komsomol	the junior section of the Party for those aged 14–28.
Tachanka	a farmer's carriage, adapted as a machine-gun transport doubling as a firing platform mounting a rear facing Maxim machine gun.
Chekists	everyday expression for a member of the secret police.
Okruzhentsy	refers specifically to those service personnel who escaped the encirclement.
Hiwi(s)	abbreviation of *Hilfswilliger*, Russian volunteer helpers working for Axis forces.
Politruk	common parlance for a unit's political officer or commissar.
Schutzmannschaften	locally raised police formations.
Lebensraum	living space, land to be cleared of its population and then repopulated with racially acceptable people.

Acronyms

NKVD	People's Commissariat for Internal Affairs, successor to the CHEKA
OMSBON	Independent/Separate Special Purpose Motorized Rifle Brigade
CHEKA	Extraordinary Commission for Combating Counterrevolution and Sabotage
CHQPM	Central Headquarters of the Partisan Movement
CPSU(b)	Communist Party of the Soviet Union (Bolshevik)
OSOAVIAKhIM	Union of Societies of Assistance to Defence and Aviation and Chemical Defence and Chemical Industry

INDEX

References to images are in bold.
References to plates are in bold
with captions in brackets.

aircraft 28
alcohol 36
ammunition 24, 25, **32**
anti-Russian sentiment 9, 41
anti-Semitism 36
appearance 19–22, 24
Axis forces 4, 5, 52, 53, 57, 58;
   and prisoners of war 7; and
   Soviet Union 8, 9

Baltic states 5, 7, 8, 9, 14, 41
Belarus 5, 8, 9, 13, 36, **60**
belonging 45
Bessarabia 5, 41
Bielski brothers 36

camp construction 38, 40, **44**
Carpathian Raid (1943) 8, 29,
   57–59
casualties 18, **33**, 60
Central HQ for the Partisan
   Movement (CHQPM) 8, 18,
   28, 32, 45
Chapaev, Vasily 5, 10
Cheka 4, 12
Chorny, Boris 4, 5, 7, 8, 29, 33,
   36; and Moscow 37; and
   patriotism 44; and recruitment
   11; and training 13, 15; and
   uniforms 22
civilians 5, 9, **11**, 13, 32, 45,
   52, 61
collaborators 10, 28, **39** (38), **49**,
   51 (50)
collectivization 12, 41–42
communications 9, 26, 28, **35**
   (34), **39** (38)
Communism 5, 29, 45
Communist Party 7, 9, 10, 11,
   12, 33
conditions of service 30–34,
   36, 61
conscription 13, 14, 15

Dargel, Paul **47** (46)
defeatists 16–17
Deliatyn, battle of (1943) 57–59
demolition **18**
deportation 12
deserters 10, 22, 36, 41
destruction battalions 10, 12,
   48, 49
discipline 36
disease 32
domestic duties 61

equipment 24–26, 28–30, 40
ethnic cleansing 45
ethnic groups 41–42, 44
executions 10, 33, **39** (38),
   40, **49**

families **9**, 31, 32
festivals 61
Finland 5, 14
flags **44**, 45
food supplies 12, **30**, 31
frontier guard 10, 11, 14–15, **17**

genocide 4, 12
Germany 9, 12, 26, 44; and exiles
   11; and Moscow 37, 38; and

uniforms 21, 22, **58**; see also
   Axis forces
'Glorious' unit 22
'Great Land' 7, 28
Guderian, Heinz 45
guerrilla warfare 7, 9, 33

Himmler, Heinrich 8
Hitler, Adolf 4, 8
homosexuality 36
hunting 13

Independent/Separate Special
   Purpose Motorised Rifle
   Brigade (OMSBON) 7, 8,
   15, 16, 61; and aircraft 28;
   and appearance 19–20, 21;
   and campaigns 37, 38, 40;
   and conditions of service 33;
   and organization 17–18;
   and patriotism 44–45; and
   recruitment 10–12
infantry scouts 14, **17**, 18
intelligence 8, 15, 22, **39** (38),
   48, **49**, 57

Jews 4, 36

Kapchinsky, Anatoly 38
KGB 4, 12
Khrushchev, Nikita 9
Kiev 7, 10, 60, 61
Koch, Erich **47** (46), 48
Komsomol 9, 11, 13
Kovpak, Sidor Artemyevitch
   7, 8, 10, 12, 24, 32, **53**,
   60; and award 61; and
   battle 36, 46, 56–57,
   58, 59; and Communism
   44–45; and equipment 28;
   and organization 30–31;
   and training 16, 17; and
   transport 29
krais 32
Kursk, battle of (1943) 8, 12, 45
Kuznetsov, Nikolai 4, 22, **25**, **47**
   (46), 48, 61

leadership 40, 45
Légion des Volontaires Français 10
Leningrad 7, 8
'Little Land' 4, 5, 12, 28, 44, 46
local knowledge 9–10
Lubyanka 4, 12

Makhno, Nestor 5
marches **15**, 48–49
medals 21, **23** (22), **59**, **60**, 61
medical units 16, **29**, 32, 60
Medvedev, Col Dmitry
   Nikolayevich 4, 11, 12, 24,
   33, 36, 45; and award 61;
   and campaigns 37–38, 52,
   53–54, 56
Minsk 8, 11, **54**, 61
'Mitya' unit 11, 12
money 29, 30
morale 32, 61
Moscow 7, 11, 26, 28, 32, 60, 61;
   defence of 16, 37, 46
Motherland 11, 13, 44
museums 61, **62**

NCOs 9, 14, 19
neutrality 12

newssheets 28
Nicholas II, Tsar of Russia 4
night exercises 16, **53**
NKVD *see* People's Commissariat
   for Internal Affairs

oath of allegiance 31
Okruzhentsy 9, 22
OMSBON *see* Independent/
   Separate Special Purpose
   Motorised Rifle Brigade
Operation *Bagration* (1944)
   8, 13, 46
Operation *Barbarossa* (1941)
   6, 7, 42
Operation *Concert* (1943) 8
Operation *Rail War* (1943) 8
organization 17–19
OSOAVIAKhIM *see* Union
   of Societies of Assistance
   to Defence and Aviation
   and Chemical Defence
   and Chemical Industry

panje wagon 29
partisan movement 4, 5–8, 12–13;
   and capability 40–41; German
   10; and organization 32–33
patriotism 44–45
People's Commissariat for Internal
   Affairs (NKVD) 7, 8, 12, 13,
   16–17, 37; and deserters 41;
   and recruitment 9, 10, 11; and
   security 19
Poles 4, 7, 11, 14
police 10, 22
Politruk 9, 19
prisoners of war (POWs) 7, 21,
   45, 49
propaganda 12, 17, 28–29, 30,
   39 (38), 61
punishment 36
Putivl (Ukraine) 7, 10, 61

radios 10, **14**, **19**, 26, 28, **35**
   (34), 40
railway lines 48, **49**, 57
rations 11
recruitment 9–13, 45–46, 48
Red Army 5, 6, 8, 13, 17, **25**, 30;
   and communication 28; and
   ethnic groups 44; and mines
   24–25; and Moscow 37; and
   organization 10; and partisans
   9, 33; and training 14
Red Army Day 32, **44**
refugees 36, 37
religion 12
report analysis 40
roadside ambushes 49–50, **51**
   (50), 52
Romania 11, 14
routines 31
Rudnev, S. V. 10, 24, 31,
   44–45, 60
rural life 36
Russian Civil War (1917–22)
   5, 10, 12, 24, 29
Russification 5, 41–42
Ruthenians 10

sabotage 13, **43** (42), 48
security 19, 57
skis 30, 41

Slavs 4, 44
slogans 18
Slovaks 10
Soviet Union 5, 6, 14–15, 32,
   41–42, 44; and traditions 61
Spadshchansky Forest 10, 61
sportsmen 11, 38
Stalin, Joseph 5, 6–7, 12, 16, 28,
   32; and ethnic groups 42, 44;
   and guerilla warfare 9
Stalingrad 8, 10, 12, 45
storage facilities 31
stragglers 9, 10, 13, 31
students 11–12
symbolism 45

tachanka 29
tasks **39** (38)
'Temporarily Occupied Territories'
   see 'Little Land'
training 13–17, 31
trans-Dnieper expedition (1942)
   56–57
transport 29, **40**, 41
Tsessarsky, Dr Albert 4, 5, 7, 8,
   19, 33, 36; and battle 50, 53;
   and casualties 60; and marches
   48; and Moscow 37; and
   recruitment 11; and training
   13–14, 15, 16

Ukraine 5, 8, 13, 17, 22, 57;
   and anti-Semitism 36; and
   collectivization 12, 41; and
   commemorations 61; and
   Koch, Erich **47** (46), 48;
   and security 19
Ukrainian Communist Party 7, 9
undercover operations **47** (46), 48
uniforms **18**, 19–22, **23** (22), 24,
   28, **29**, **39** (38), **58**
Union of Societies of Assistance
   to Defence and Aviation
   and Chemical Defence
   and Chemical Industry
   (OSOAVIAKhIM) 13, 21
USSR *see* Soviet Union

Vershigora, P. P. 56, 57, 59
volunteers 9–10, 11, 12–13,
   30, 37
'Voroshilov' unit 40, 56

Warsaw 5, 13
weaponry, Axis **27** (26)
weaponry, Soviet 15, 16, **23** (22),
   30, **31**, **34**, **55** (54); anti-tank
   rifles **37**, 40; carbines **60**;
   detonators **58**; hand grenades
   17, **36**; machine guns **16**, 17,
   24, 25, 28, **41**, 50, 52, 53;
   mines 24–25, 30, 38, **43** (42),
   48, 49, 57; Molotov cocktails
   15, 50; mortars **16**; revolvers
   25–26, **32**; rifles 24, 40
weather conditions 13, 15, 28, 32
weddings **34**, 36
'Winners' unit 11, 18, **19**, 29, 33,
   34, 36; and battle 46, 48–50,
   52–54, 56, 57; and campaigns
   37–38; and uniform 21, 24
women **15**, 20, 36
World War I (1914–18) 10, 44